Missouri

AMERICA THE BEAUTIFUL

second series

Missouri

Martin Hintz

Children's Press®
A Division of Scholastic Inc.
New York • Toronto • London • Auckland • Sydney
Mexico City • New Delhi • Hong Kong
Danbury, Connecticut

Frontispiece: Scenic Missouri sunset
Front cover: Gateway Arch, St. Louis
Back cover: Ozarks cabin

Consultant: Therese Bigelow, Kansas City Public Library

Please note: All statistics are as up-to-date as possible at the time of publication.

Book production by Editorial Directions, Inc.

Library of Congress Cataloging-in-Publication Data

Hintz, Martin.
Missouri / by Martin Hintz.
144 p. 24 cm. — (America the beautiful. Second series)
Includes bibliographical references (p.) and index.
Summary : Describes the geography, plants, animals, history, economy, language, religions, culture, sports, arts, and people of the state of Missouri.
ISBN 0-516-20836-5
1. Missouri—Juvenile literature. [1. Missouri.] I. Title. II. Series.
F466.3.H56 1999
977.8—dc21 98-27785
CIP
AC

Printed in the United States of America
3 4 5 6 7 8 9 0 R 08 07 06 05 04 03 02 01

Acknowledgments

For their insight, suggestions, and editorial assistance, the author wishes to thank Jim Gardner, director of communications for the Missouri Department of Economic Development; Eddie G. Davis, president, St. Louis Minority Business Council; Steve Kappler, Missouri Division of Tourism; Nancy Milton and Donna Andrews of the St. Louis Convention & Visitors Commission; and other tourism officials on both the state and local levels; the staff of the Missouri Department of Natural Resources; Kate Graf, reference librarian, Missouri State Library; and Lori Simms, Bob Muldoon, and Andrea O'Brien.

Canoeing on the Mehemec River

The Gateway Arch

W. C. Handy

Contents

Mark McGwire

Maya Angelou

The Mississippi River

A honeybee

A bluebird

Chapter One

Versions of Missouri

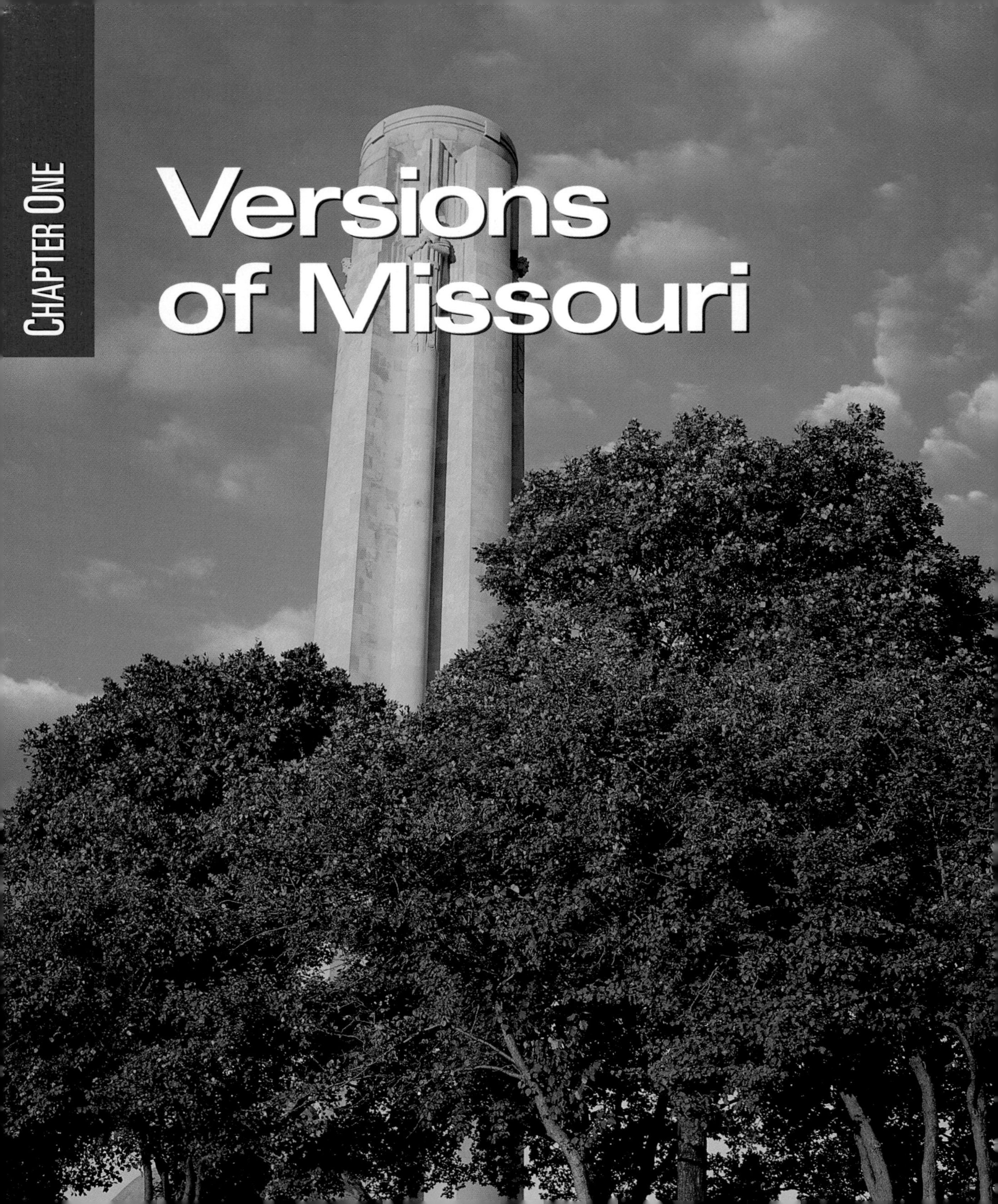

Trail of Tears State Park

There is a problem in Missouri. It's not a major challenge, but a problem nonetheless. The question is: How do you pronounce the state's name? Do you say Missour-EE or Missour-AH?

The Native Americans, of course, had their own reference for this land, one that is rich in natural resources. Long ago, warriors of the Fox nation met a tribe who lived along the *mesis-piya*—the Mississippi River. The Fox called the other Indians the *Oumessourit*, meaning the "Big-Canoe People," because they were skilled canoe builders who lived along the mighty river. And so the root of

Opposite: Liberty Memorial

Geopolitical map of Missouri

the state's official name was formed. But no one is exactly sure how the Indians pronounced *Missouri*.

The Spanish and French probably put their own twist on that word when they colonized the region. Then came Scotch-Irish settlers from the eastern United States. Students of language say that the Missouri "hill twang" spoken in the Ozarks by these settlers is the closest we can come to hearing the English language as playwright William Shakespeare might have spoken it centuries ago.

The Scotch-Irish were followed into Missouri by people of many other nationalities. They each had their own particular way of speaking, all of which influenced how *Missouri* was pronounced.

French and Scotch-Irish settlers often interacted around St. Louis.

Good-Natured Arguments

Since the early 1800s, Missourians have argued good-naturedly—usually—over this question of pronunciation. It is the ideal debate topic—both sides are right and both sides are wrong.

A few years ago, when members of the Automobile Club of Missouri voted on their choice of pronunciation, 66 percent preferred the "ee" ending. The eastern half of the state agreed. The vote broke even along age lines. A majority of residents under forty-five said Missour-EE. Yet many western Missourians say they live in Missour-AH, with a Missour-UH sneaking in there sometimes.

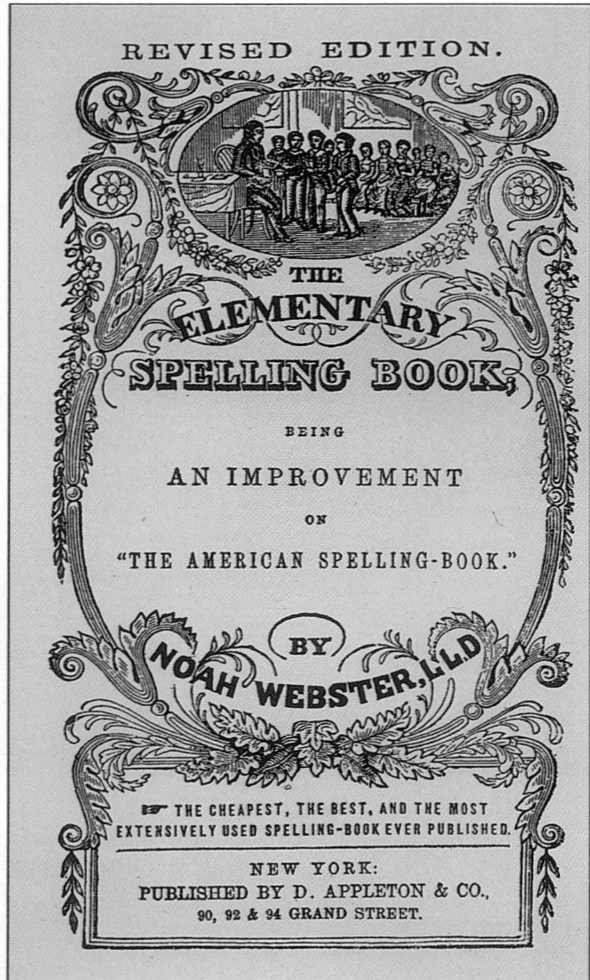
REVISED EDITION.

THE ELEMENTARY SPELLING BOOK;

BEING

AN IMPROVEMENT

ON

"THE AMERICAN SPELLING-BOOK."

BY

NOAH WEBSTER, LL.D.

☞ THE CHEAPEST, THE BEST, AND THE MOST EXTENSIVELY USED SPELLING-BOOK EVER PUBLISHED.

NEW YORK:
PUBLISHED BY D. APPLETON & CO.,
90, 92 & 94 GRAND STREET.

Noah Webster's spelling book offered one solution to the pronunciation question.

In 1783, Noah Webster's "spelling book" offered one solution. He wrote, "The true pronunciation of the name of a place is that which prevails in and near the place." Okay. Now what do you think is the best pronunciation?

Other sounds that reveal the flavor of Missouri include the sharp cry of a grouse in the Mark Twain National Forest, the rumble of a truck on Interstate 44 outside St. James, and the lonely wail of a night train leaving Warrenton. Then there's the swish of a broom on a porch in Trenton, the laughter of kids playing baseball in Harrisonville, the cry of a saxophone coming from a St. Louis jazz club, and the preaching of a sermon in Albany.

Earning a Nickname

These sounds serve as the background for a people who traditionally have their own way of doing things. This attitude has been called "stubbornness" by some and "pride" by others. Whichever it is, Missouri is nicknamed the Show-Me State.

Although it is not official, the phrase is used on the state's automobile license plates. There are several ideas on how the term came to be. The best-known legend attributes the comment to Congressman Willard Duncan Vandiver, who served in the U.S.

Missouri license plate

House of Representatives from 1897 to 1903. During a speech, he declared, "I come from a state that raises corn and cotton and cockleburs and Democrats, and frothy eloquence neither convinces nor satisfies me. I am from Missouri. You have got to show me."

Another version says that a group of Missouri miners went to Colorado as strikebreakers in the mid-1890s, but they were not familiar with the western techniques of drilling. The pit bosses had to say, "That man is from Missouri. You'll have to show him."

Whatever the origin, the phrase now means that level-headed Missourians need hard action to convince them. Today, Missourians are convinced that their state, no matter how they pronounce its name, is a good place to be.

Chapter Two

The Good Old Days

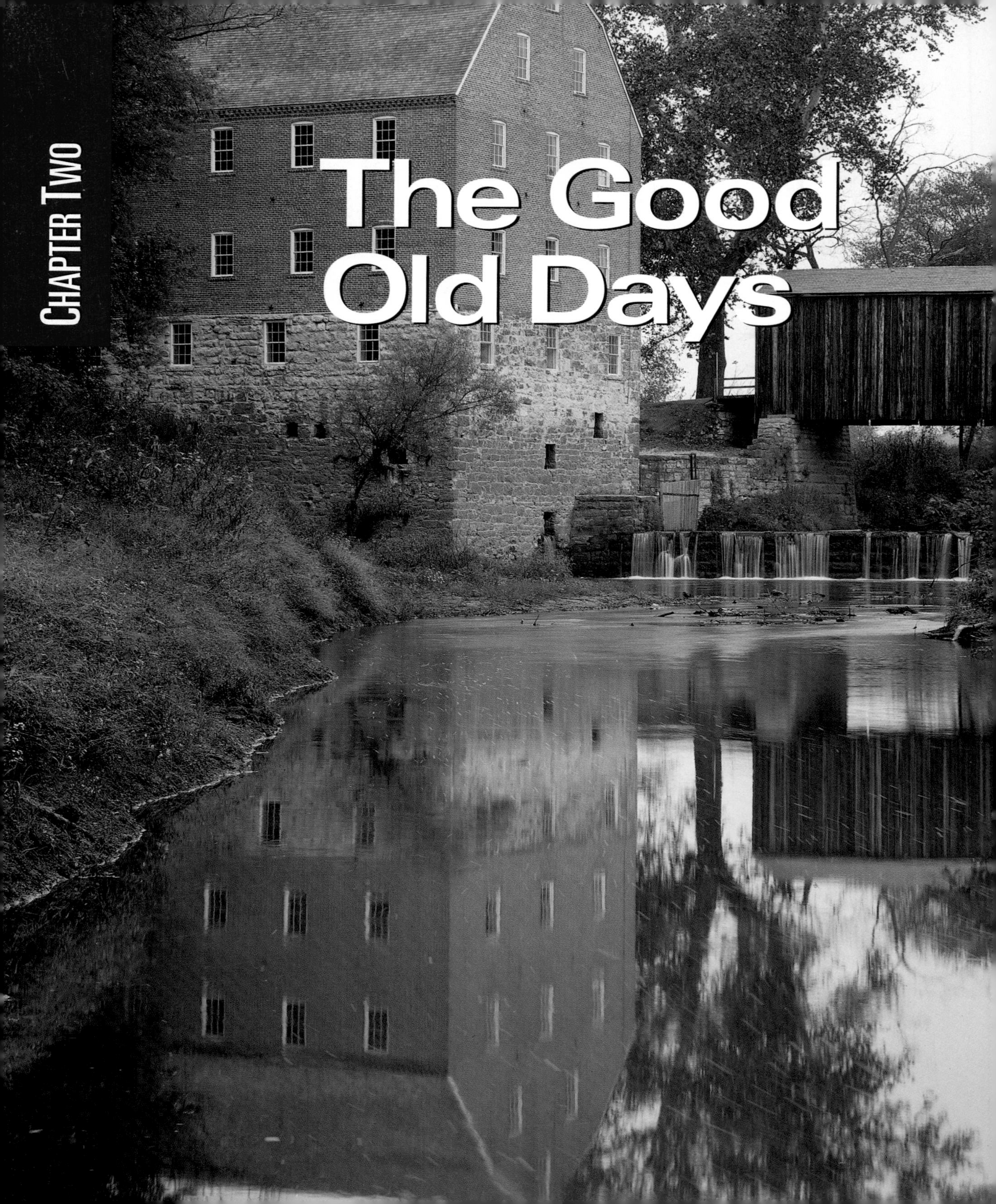

Lake of the Ozarks State Park is one place where cultures crossed paths.

Imagine hiking along a high ridgeline in far southern Missouri. A slight breeze ruffles the dried oak leaves. The drumming of a woodpecker echoes far off in the forest while a red-tailed hawk soars high overhead. No one else seems to be nearby.

But you are not alone. Spirits of long-ago ancients surround you. For at least 10,000 years, Missouri has been a crossroads for many tribes of Native Americans. They all left their mark on the state. Their trails became highways, and their legends became part of Missouri folklore. Their names became city names. Wherever you go in Missouri, someone has been there before.

Nomads and Mound Builders

The earliest Missourians were skilled nomadic hunters. Always on the go, they tracked the migrating herds of elk and bison that roamed the prehistoric landscape. The first people to live permanently in one spot are now called the Bluff Shelter People. More than 2,000 years ago, they huddled in shallow caves on the edge of rivers, where it was easy to fish. They made simple fishhooks, awls, and axes from stone and bone, planted crops, and built canoes. Sometimes, they broke a clay bowl or misplaced a spear

Opposite: Bollinger Mill

The Giant Mound

The largest mound in Missouri is in Pemiscot County near Caruthersville. It is 400 feet (122 m) long, 250 feet (76 m) wide, and 35 feet (11 m) high. Originally, the sides were covered with burnt clay from 3 to 5 inches (7.6 to 12.7 cm) thick. Split cane was laid between the layers of clay. This earthen structure was probably the base for a temple, but no one is absolutely sure of its purpose. ■

point. Today's archaeologists have found shards, or pieces, of their pots and other artifacts.

Much later, other early people built mounds along the banks of the Missouri and Mississippi Rivers, many of which can still be seen from Cape Girardeau south to northern Arkansas. Some mounds were used for burials, and others must have had a different religious significance. The people traded extensively with other villages, in an economic network reaching from the East Coast to the Gulf of Mexico.

The heart of the mound builders' culture was at Cahokia, Illinois. Just across the Mississippi River, in the area now called St. Louis, were many other mounds, which is why St. Louis was originally called Mound City. The mound-building Missourians faded into time's secret mist about 1,500 years ago, and their mounds have since been leveled for modern buildings.

After the mysterious mound builders came the peoples of the Woodland and Mississippi cultures. Telling the difference between these two is relatively easy. The Woodland people made pottery in only one shape and buried their dead without any artifacts—tools, weapons, or other implements. They began to stay in one place and farm the land.

The Mississippians had a variety of pottery styles, and they placed cooking utensils, knives, and other items in their graves. They probably believed a person's spirit needed these things in the next life. These people gathered in clusters that began to resemble towns.

Eventually these long-ago Missourians also disappeared. Perhaps they were driven away by the ancestors of the Native Ameri-

Decorated pottery of the mound builders

can people who were there when the European explorers arrived. Or perhaps they merged with other Native American peoples.

The Native American Nations

Several different nations of Native Americans lived in Missouri in more recent centuries. The Sauk, Fox, and Illinois lived in the northeastern part of the state. The Oto, Iowa, Missouri, Quapaw, and Kansa lived elsewhere in the region. They farmed the rich soil, hunted in the dense forests, and fished the cool streams. The Osage occupied more than a quarter of what is now Missouri. They were the strongest and largest of these groups, not just in numbers but in the size of the people. The men often were taller than 6 feet (180 cm), and some reached 7 feet (210 cm)!

Later, other Indian groups such as the Shawnee and Delaware filtered into the area. They had been forced westward by the growing numbers of white settlers in the East, as well as by more warlike Indian neighbors.

Hernando de Soto crossing the Mississippi

It is possible that gold-seeking Spanish troops commanded by Hernando de Soto traded with Indians living in Missouri as early as 1541. His well-equipped expedition, with its fierce war dogs, guns, and metal armor, traveled from Florida to the Mississippi River. About the same time, Francisco Vásquez de Coronado trekked up from Mexico. Along the way, both expeditions met Native Americans. Missouri's native population may have been among them.

The French Empire

The first recorded contact of white men and natives came from the French. In May 1673, French explorer Louis Jolliet and Father Jacques Marquette, a Roman Catholic priest, left what is now Green Bay, Wisconsin. Their long canoe trip took them down the Wisconsin River to the Mississippi. They got to where the Mississippi and Missouri Rivers meet before returning north to French headquarters in Quebec, Canada. They took with them tales of giant catfish, huge bison, and an open land just waiting to be explored.

In 1682, René-Robert Cavelier, Sieur de La Salle, used the same river route as trailblazers Jolliet and Marquette. Accompanied by twenty-three Europeans and twenty-eight Indians, the ambitious

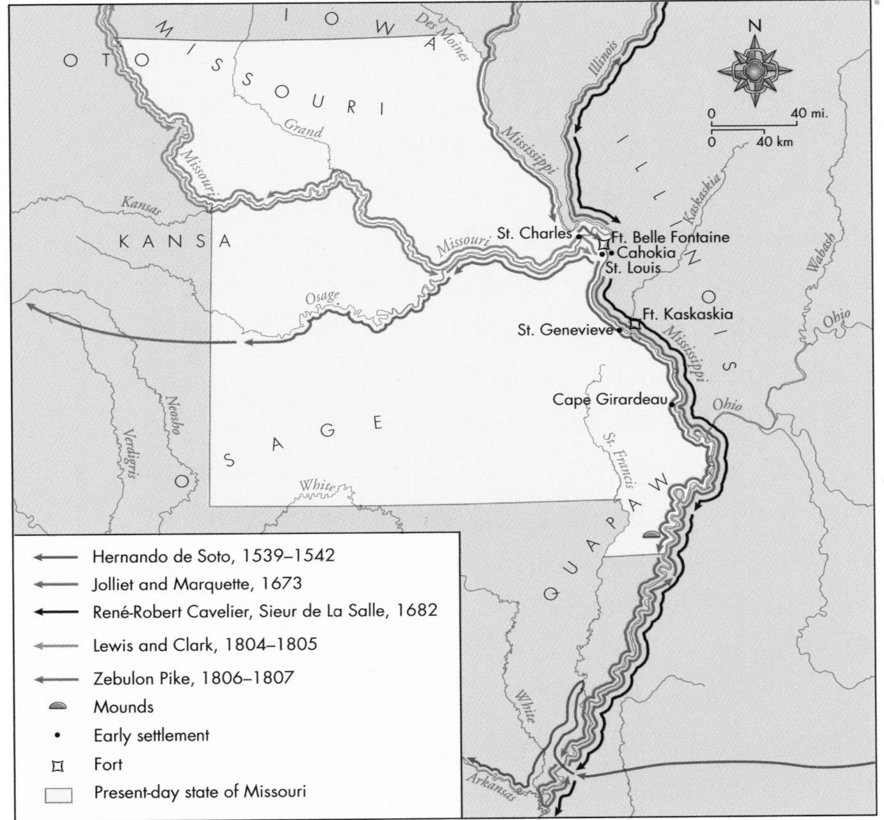

Exploration of Missouri

Louis Jolliet and Jacques Marquette's expedition in 1673

adventurer claimed for France all the land drained by the Mississippi River and its tributaries. He named this vast territory *Louisiana* after King Louis XIV of France.

Other explorers, priests, soldiers, and settlers followed. France's sprawling American empire soon reached from Canada's St. Lawrence River to the Gulf of Mexico.

The French considered both banks of the Mississippi River as their "Illinois" section of Louisiana. They built settlements at Cahokia in 1699 and Kaskaskia in 1703, in what is now Illinois just across the river from today's St. Louis. In 1703, Father Gabriel Marest established the village of St. Francis Xavier at the mouth of the River des Peres on the west bank of the Mississippi River. Although this village lasted only about two years, it is considered the first white settlement in what would become Missouri. If it still existed, it would be within the city of St. Louis.

The Illinois–Missouri portion of the Louisiana territory proved to be an important piece of real estate. Fur trade with the Native Americans steadily developed into a booming industry for the French. There was also a frenzied search for silver beginning in 1720, fueled by rumors of treasure brought back to France by some explorers. French miners and their African slaves scrambled across Missouri's hills in the eastern Ozark Mountains looking for the elusive metal. All they found was lead, but that metal proved to be just as important as silver because it was used in making bullets.

Ste. Genevieve

Getting the Lead Out

Philip Renault was an early lead miner in Missouri. He smelted, or melted, the ore found by his miners and poured it into molds shaped like horse collars. The purified lead was then loaded onto pack mules and hauled to Fort de Chartres in Illinois. Later, Renault switched to carts and built a network of crude roads to get his lead to market. This was Missouri's first "highway" system. ■

Early in the 1730s, a few French families from Kaskaskia crossed the Mississippi River to settle on the west bank. They named the site Ste. Genevieve. This became the first permanent white settlement in Missouri. The modern town of Ste. Genevieve still celebrates its French heritage with the *Jour de Fête* (Party Day) art festival and the King's Ball.

Spain Takes Over

The New World was always at the mercy of Old World politics. In 1762, France secretly gave Spain its Louisiana territory west of the Mississippi River. Spain had been France's ally in Europe's Seven

Governor Gayuso, who presided over lower Louisana

Years' War, which was won by England. In North America, this bloody confrontation was called the French and Indian War.

The Seven Years' War officially ended with the Treaty of Paris, signed in 1763. The treaty required France to give up most of the rest of its possessions in North America. It gave Canada and the Louisiana territory east of the Mississippi River to England.

French adventurers in the New World paid little attention to what was going on in Europe, however. In 1764, traders set up shop on a western bluff overlooking the Mississippi. One of the traders, Pierre Laclède, built log houses and a trading post on the site. It was turned into a village by Auguste Chouteau, who named the community *St. Louis* in honor of King Louis IX, who had been made a saint.

The Spanish divided their new territory on the western side of the river into Lower and Upper Louisiana. The king of Spain appointed a governor who resided in New Orleans. In turn, that official appointed a lieutenant governor, who was based in St. Louis, to oversee Upper Louisiana. Since there were few Spaniards in the region, the residents kept on using French language, customs, and trading practices with the Indians.

When the American Revolution broke out in 1775, the French and Spanish throughout Louisiana sided with the colonists. Helped by soldiers from St. Louis, American general George Rogers Clark drove out the English troops stationed in Illinois. This safeguarded the western frontier for the rebel colonies.

When the American Revolution ground to a bloody halt in 1783, Britain granted the spread of prairie and forestland between the Appalachian Mountains and the Mississippi River to the new United States. Settlers immediately flooded into the newly opened territory. The Spanish, on the other side of the river, were afraid that if the Americans decided to cross the river into Missouri, nothing could stop them.

Gone for Good

On May 26, 1780, a small group of English soldiers and a thousand Indian allies tried to capture St. Louis. Captain Fernando de Leyba and fifty brave Spanish soldiers were aided by the sharpshooting citizens of the young city in driving back the attackers. If the English had been successful, they would have regained control over much of the land along the Mississippi River.

To avoid trouble, Spain offered grants of land and promised religious freedom to anyone who became a Spanish citizen. Even the famous frontiersman Daniel Boone of Kentucky took advantage of the offer. He was made a *syndic*—a Spanish judge—and lived there the last years of his life. By 1803, more than 10,000 Americans had settled near St. Louis, Cape Girardeau, St. Charles, and other eastern Missouri towns. Many African-Americans, both slave and free, crossed the Mississippi into America's western frontier.

An Amazing Bargain

Again, events in Europe affected Missouri. In Spain, officials felt that far-off Louisiana was becoming more of a problem than a benefit. At the same time, French dictator Napoleon Bonaparte wanted to rebuild his American empire. So, under the 1800 Treaty of San Ildefonso, the Spanish gave Louisiana back to the French in exchange for the principality of Tuscany in Italy.

Napoleon Bonaparte, who sold Louisiana to the United States

Then, when Napoleon needed money to fight his European wars, he offered to sell the entire area to the United States for $15 million. President Thomas Jefferson agreed. In 1803, under the terms of the Louisiana Purchase, Missouri became part of the United States.

Historical map of Missouri

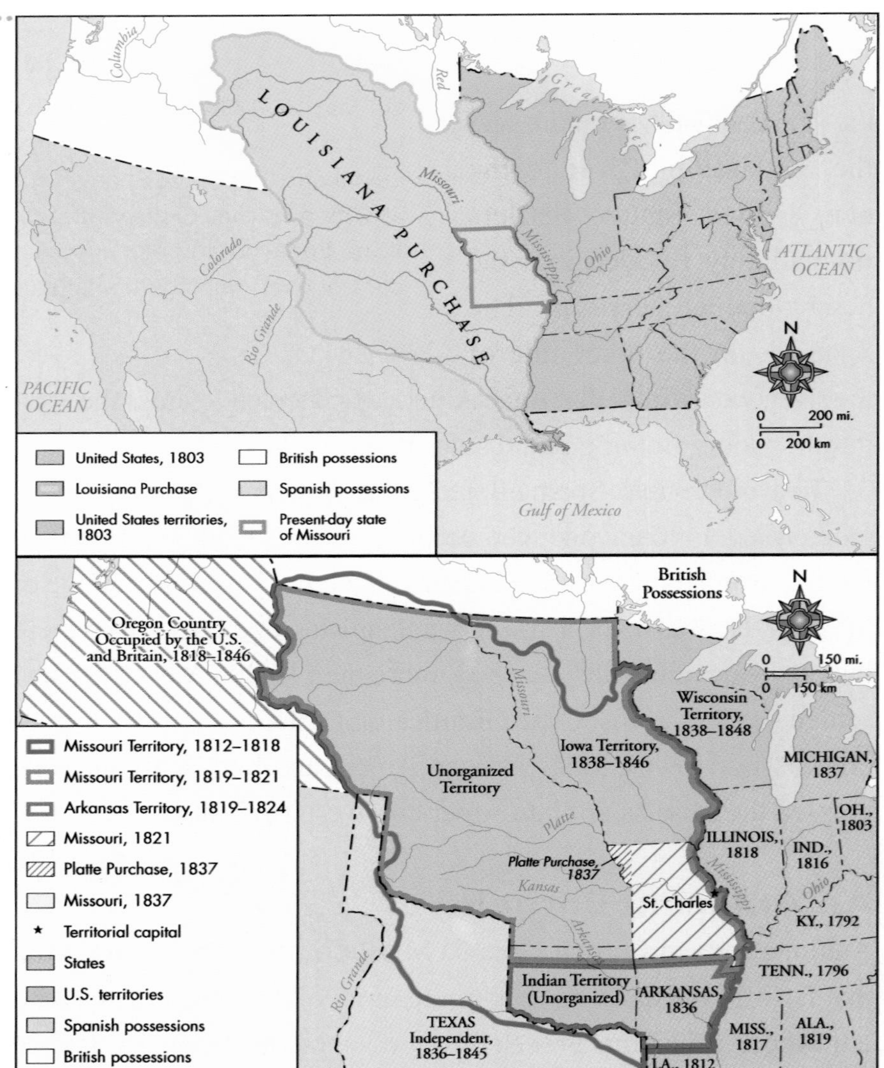

Bollinger Mill

When George Bollinger came from North Carolina to Missouri in 1797, he received a 649-acre (263-ha) land grant from the Spanish commander at Cape Girardeau. In exchange for the land, Bollinger brought in other settlers from the East, including his six brothers and their families. They settled along the Whitewater River in southeastern Missouri and built several grain mills. The Bollinger Mill State Historic Site near Jackson reminds visitors of that era.

Territory Divided

The U.S. Congress divided its huge new Louisiana Purchase lands into two sections in 1804. The southern section became the Territory of Orleans and the northern section, which included Missouri, became the District of Louisiana (later named the Louisiana Territory).

The Louisiana Purchase was a vast territory that followed the Missouri River into unknown lands. President Thomas Jefferson decided that explorers needed to investigate the land he had bought.

The New Flag Is Raised

On March 9, 1804, the U.S. Army formally took possession of Missouri. Captain Amos Stoddard raised the American flag in St. Louis to make the transfer of power official. Many of the longtime French residents were sorry to see the French flag descend, but others were just as glad to become American citizens.

In 1804, Jefferson sent Captain Meriwether Lewis and Lieutenant William Clark to head an expedition to explore the new land. Departing from St. Louis, they sailed up the Missouri River, crossed the Great Plains, and rafted down the Columbia River. At its mouth, they saw the Pacific Ocean. They were gone for two and a half years, but their reports, when they returned to St. Louis, excited everyone.

The mighty Missouri River was a convenient, though often stormy, pathway into the interior of new U.S. territory. That fact brought many adventurers and businesspeople to the region, particularly to St. Louis, where the river meets the Mississippi.

As the number of residents increased, Missouri's status as a separate territory was made official in 1812. A legislature was elected, with the governor named by the president. Only white males who had lived in the territory for a year were allowed to vote.

William Clark (left) and Meriwether Lewis

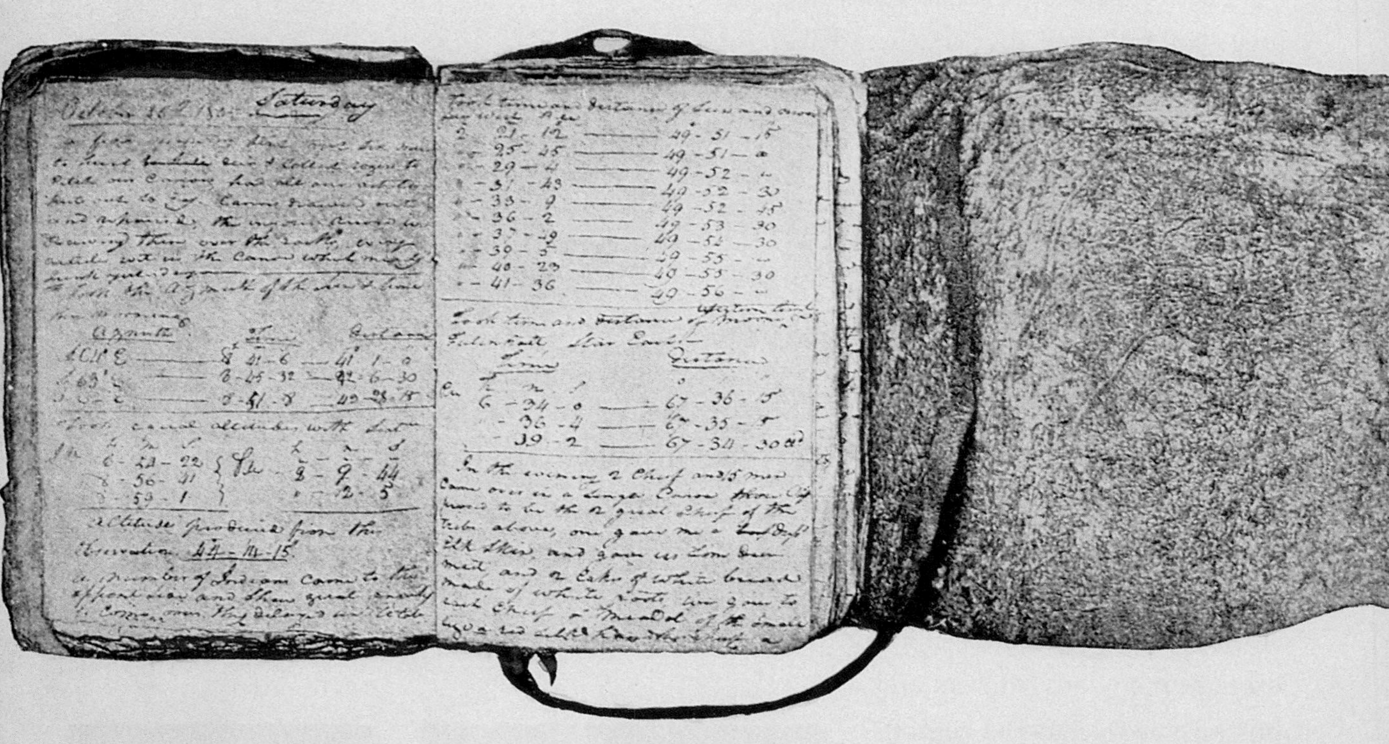

Two Men from Virginia

Meriwether Lewis (1774–1809) was born in Virginia, where he began managing his family's plantation at age eighteen. He joined the U.S. Army in 1794 and served at several frontier posts. Lewis and his neighbor, Thomas Jefferson, were good friends, and Lewis became his secretary when Jefferson was elected president.

In 1804, Jefferson appointed Lewis head of the expedition to explore the Louisiana Purchase. Lewis invited William Clark, a fellow Virginian, to share the leadership. The journals of their adventures still make for exciting reading (above).

After returning from the West, Lewis was made governor of the Louisiana Territory. However, in 1809 while journeying back to Washington, D.C., to give a report, he was found dead in an inn in Tennessee. It is not certain whether he was murdered or committed suicide.

William Clark (1770–1838) was made superintendent of Indian Affairs by President Jefferson, remaining in St. Louis. He later served as territorial governor of Missouri and lived in St. Louis until his death. ■

Establishing a Balance

Governor Alexander McNair

Missouri's request for statehood in 1818 sparked a fierce debate and a national crisis. If Missouri were admitted as a state where slavery was allowed, it would upset the balance of power in Congress between slave states and free states. The problem was resolved by the Missouri Compromise of 1820. Missouri was allowed to enter the United States as a slave state and Maine would enter the Union as the balancing free state. Congress divided the rest of the Louisiana Territory, with slavery prohibited north of 36° 31', so that other states formed from the Louisiana Purchase would maintain the balance.

Immediately, delegates were elected to attend a state constitutional convention in St. Louis. In thirty-two days, a document was drawn up that defined the role of the governor, general assembly, and judiciary. Slavery was recognized, but slaves could be given their freedom and laws were written to provide for their humane treatment. Alexander McNair, a well-known farmer, was elected the state's first governor.

After some last-minute wrangling over a few technicalities, the U.S. Congress approved Missouri's new constitution. On August 10, 1821, President James Monroe proclaimed Missouri the twenty-fourth state.

Steps to Statehood

1803—Under the Louisiana Purchase, Missouri becomes part of the United States.

1812—Missouri has enough residents to became an independent territory. A House of Representatives is elected and a governor is chosen by the president.

1818—Missouri applies for statehood.

1820—The Missouri Compromise paves the way for Missouri to become a slave state and Maine to become a free state. Alexander McNair is the first elected governor and senators are chosen.

August 10, 1821—Missouri is admitted to the Union as the twenty-fourth state.

Chapter Three

Movin' On

Sauk and Fox Indians often met in Missouri.

Missouri suffered growing pains as a young state. Borders were juggled before today's boundaries were finalized. At statehood, the "Boot Heel" region of southeastern Missouri was grafted onto the state. This was the result of the efforts of a wealthy planter named J. Hardeman Walker who lived in the area. He loved Missouri—and probably figured he could get some tax breaks too if he lived in the state. The Boot Heel includes Pemiscot and Dunklin Counties.

The Platte Purchase of 1837 brought in another 3,000 square miles (7,770 sq km) east of the Missouri River near the mouth of the Kansas River. This parcel of land was brought into Missouri

Opposite: Passengers on a steamboat at the Louisiana Purchase Exposition of 1904

The Peculiar New Madrid Bend

Ever-changing waterways and shifting sandbars along Missouri's borders caused many problems over the years. One of the most unusual was a mixed-up boundary that was hotly contested in 1859.

At the border between Kentucky and Tennessee, where these states look across the Mississippi River at Missouri, is a small, almost circular peninsula of land surrounded on all sides except the south by the river and, consequently, by Missouri. The 7,000-acre (2,835-hectare) area, called the New Madrid Bend, is cotton-growing land. This land belongs to Kentucky today, but its residents have to get to their homes through Tennessee on the south. ■

because of tension between settlers and the Sauk, Fox, and Potawatomi Indians who used the area for hunting. When the Indians finally gave up their land claims, more settlers poured into the region. This land became the counties of Platte, Buchanan, Andrew, Holt, Atchison, and Nodaway.

Land Disputes

At first, even Missouri's northern boundary with Iowa was not fixed. A controversy over language in a land survey caused so much tension between the two states that their militias were called up, with the possibility that they might fight each other. At issue was about 2,600 square miles (6,734 sq km) of land. The U.S. Supreme Court ruled that the land belonged to Iowa.

The Mormon Wars

Land disputes were often bloody. In 1831, Joseph Smith, founder of the Church of Jesus Christ of Latter-day Saints—also known as the Mormons—moved his followers to western Missouri. They settled

A battle between Mormons and non-Mormons at Haun's Mill

in the Independence area and kept to themselves. The Mormons were prosperous farmers who were strongly opposed to slavery.

Within a few short years, as more Mormons moved to the area, the balance of political power shifted in their favor. This frightened the local non-Mormon community. Gunfights broke out in Clay, Daviess, and Caldwell counties in what was called the Mormon Wars. In 1838, Governor Lilburn W. Boggs ordered the militia to chase the Mormons out of the state.

After a sojourn at Nauvoo in Illinois, where Smith was murdered, the group moved west. Most of the Mormons, under Brigham Young, settled in Utah, far from persecution. The others, who called themselves the Reorganized Church of Jesus Christ of Latter-day Saints, moved back to Independence. They established their church headquarters there in 1904.

Westward, Ho!

The city of Independence, near Kansas City, was the starting point for some of the most famous wagon-train routes to the West. The Santa Fe Trail, opened about 1821, began as a merchants' trail to New Mexico. The Oregon Trail, used by fur traders to reach the Columbia River, became a busy highway of wagon trains in the 1840s for the many settlers seeking new land in the Northwest.

The Maturing State

As trade and settlement increased, Missouri slowly put aside its rough-and-ready frontier ways. Day-to-day life became more "civilized." The Bank of Missouri, chartered in 1837, was the first strong financial institution in the state. Two years later, a state superintendent of schools was hired and the state university system established.

The young state was on the go. Population exploded and commerce expanded. Wagon trains rolled through Missouri on their way to the rich farmlands farther west. Meanwhile, patriotic Missourians quickly rallied to help the country when there was trouble. They provided most of the manpower for the U.S. Western Army during the Mexican War (1846–1848). The conflict, which cost more than 11,000 U.S. lives, was fought between the territory-hungry United States and Mexico, its southern neighbor.

Prelude to Civil War

Throughout this era, the conflict between Americans over the issue of slavery was increasing. Some Missourians hinted that they might secede, or withdraw, from the Union if war broke out

A Missouri Slave and National Division

Dred Scott was a slave who once lived in Illinois and Minnesota, both of which were free states in the tumultuous era before the American Civil War (1861–1865). In 1838, Scott's owner took him back to Missouri. After his master died in 1846, Scott sued for his liberty. He argued that his residency in free states made him a citizen.

The Missouri Supreme Court ruled that Scott returned to the state on his own and voluntarily resumed slavery. Of course, Scott and his supporters did not agree with this, and the case made its way to the U.S. Supreme Court. Scott lost the decision because the justices said that since Scott was a slave, he was not a citizen of Missouri and thus could not sue in federal courts. The case solidified the position that slavery was legal in parts of the United States and that slaves had no rights. This decision contributed to the bitterness leading to the Civil War.

over slavery. Even powerful politicians such as Senator Thomas Hart Benton of Missouri were caught up in the fray. Benton had earlier been in favor of slavery, but when he realized that it was tearing the nation apart, he started to crusade against slavery expansion. His new realization caused a split in Missouri's Democratic Party and ended Benton's thirty-year career in Congress.

In 1855, thousands of proslavery Missourians, called Border Ruffians, crossed into Kansas, where they helped elect lawmakers who legalized slavery. Antislavery forces, nicknamed Jayhawkers, then selected their own legislature and asked Congress to admit Kansas into the Union as a free state. Soon, open warfare broke out along the Missouri-Kansas border. By the time the fighting between Ruffians and Jayhawkers ended, more than 200 people had died.

Advocates of slavery crossing into Kansas

Anger was mounting, building toward a larger conflict. In 1860, one out of eleven people in Missouri was a slave, for a total of 107,456 enslaved African-Americans. Two-thirds of them lived in only a few areas along the Mississippi River. The state's urban areas were mostly antislavery. But feelings still ran high between the proslavery and antislavery factions, especially after six Southern states seceded from the Union and formed a new nation called the Confederate States of America. Five other states joined the Confederacy later, but Missouri was not among them.

Tensions rose as different militia units were formed on behalf of the Union and Confederate groups. When the Civil War broke out in April 1861, federal troops were called out to protect the government arsenal in St. Louis. Governor Claiborne F. Jackson

Troops leaving Boonville after Jackson's defeat

responded by requesting 50,000 Missourians to repel what he called the Union invasion. Jackson's poorly equipped men were defeated at the Battle of Boonville on June 17.

Battleground

Then in October 1861, Jackson called for a session of the legislature, and because there were not enough legislators attending to hold a legal session, those present voted to join the Confederacy. This division between the Union and Confederate sides in Missouri led it into an era of bloodshed. In July 1861, the pro-Union forces took control of the state, and Governor Jackson was replaced by Hamilton R. Gamble.

There were no major Civil War battles in Missouri, but over a thousand bloody skirmishes were fought there, more than in any other state except Virginia and Tennessee. Most of these battles occurred when Southern sympathizers tried to take the state away from Union sympathizers. Brother fought brother as 40,000 Missourians joined the Confederate forces and 110,000 enlisted in the Union Army. By the time the war ended, more than 27,000 Missourians had died.

A Long Time Recovering

Life was not easy in Missouri after the Civil War. Men who had fought one another suddenly had to be partners in building their state. It was difficult to put aside their hatreds.

The Battle of Wilson's Creek

An important battle took place along Wilson's Creek, near Springfield, on August 10, 1861. The troops of former Missouri governor Sterling Price, who had become a Confederate general, took on those of Union general Nathaniel Lyon. Price hoped to recapture Missouri and hand the state over to the Confederacy. Lyon became the first Union general to die in battle, and the Union troops were forced to retreat, but Price and his men failed to follow up, so the battle was really a draw. The battlefield at Wilson's Creek is now a National Battlefield Park. ■

The James Boys

Jesse (left) and Frank (right) James of Centerville (now called Kearney) were among the most colorful outlaws in Missouri after the Civil War. The James Boys led a gang that robbed and burned its way across the Midwest, getting as far north as Northfield, Minnesota. They robbed at least fourteen banks, the Kansas City Fair, and numerous trains. Missouri's governor Thomas T. Crittenden and several railroads offered huge sums of money for their capture.

Bob Ford and his brother Charles belonged to the hard-riding James gang, but loyalty did not mean anything compared with reward money. Because of his friendship with Jesse James, Bob Ford was able to gain access to the gang's hideout in St. Joseph. On April 3, 1882, Ford shot Jesse in the back. The Fords immediately surrendered to the police. They went on trial and were sentenced to be hanged. Governor Crittenden pardoned the two men amidst accusations that he had contracted the killing.

Frank James—never found guilty of anything—ended his days quietly. He turned himself in and lived to be seventy-two years old, dying quietly in February 18, 1915, on the family farm at Kearney. Frank sometimes earned money by appearing in carnival sideshows and telling of his adventures. It was certainly a long way from his wilder days as a young man. ■

Some former soldiers found themselves expert in warfare but with no hope of finding a job in a distressed economy. Some of them turned to crime to make a living. In 1874, Missouri's first recorded train robbery occurred at Gad's Hill in Wayne County.

Most Missourians tried to put their differences aside and look to the future. A new state constitution outlawed slavery and emphasized education. It said that at least 25 percent of the state's general revenue was to be used to maintain public schools.

The state's newspapers led the way in influencing public opinion about the people's welfare and democratic ideals. The *Kansas City Star*, *St. Louis Globe-Democrat*, *St. Louis Journal,* and other publications became known for their feisty editorials and investigations of corruption. Author Lincoln Steffens wrote that St. Louis had one of the most corrupt city governments of the postwar era in the United States. His digging for facts helped reformers clean house.

Life had changed after the war. Railroads crisscrossed the frontier, so there were no more wagon trains needing supplies from Missouri's warehouses.

Famed Journalist Establishes Writing Prize

Joseph Pulitzer, a Hungarian-born reporter, purchased the *St. Louis Post* and the *St. Louis Dispatch* in 1878, merging them in 1880. He turned the *St. Louis Post-Dispatch* into one of the most respected papers in the United States. Pulitzer moved to New York and enlarged his newspaper empire by buying other newspapers. Wherever he was, Pulitzer fought for civil reform and demanded clean government. The Pulitzer Prizes, named after this famous publisher, are still the nation's most prestigious journalism and literary awards. ■

The fur trade was gone too, and the damaged and workerless plantations were broken into small farms. Life was tough.

To protect their interests, Missouri's farmers banded together in the Grange, the Agricultural Wheel, and other political and social organizations. Workers in the cities went on strike for better wages and shorter working hours.

In the late 1880s, Cubans revolted against Spain, which controlled the Caribbean island, and tales of atrocities encouraged Missourians to want to help. Many volunteered to join the U.S. military. The Spanish-American War broke out in 1898 in Cuba and other Spanish-held territories. Although no complete Missouri units actually fought in Cuba, many state soldiers were in the thick of the fighting. Frank Fulton planted the first U.S. flag on San Juan Hill, in one of the war's most famous battles, and Edward P. Stanton was the first soldier to raise the flag over Manila Bay in the Philippines, at which U.S. vessels destroyed ten Spanish ships. Both men were from St. Louis.

The American flag being raised on Cuban soil in 1898

Meet Me in St. Louis

St. Louis decided to strut its stuff with a World's Fair, opening in 1904, in celebration of the 100th anniversary of the Louisiana Purchase. The Louisiana Purchase Exposition, the fair's official name, was a great success, favorably portraying Missouri as a forward-looking state. The most popular song of the era was the fair's hit theme song, "Meet Me in St. Louie, Louie." Missouri writer Sally Benson later wrote a movie about the fair, starring Judy Garland, called *Meet Me in St. Louis.*

An estimated 20 million people came to the fairgrounds to tour the international pavilions, see the Palace of Electricity, and sample new taste treats called ice cream cones and iced tea. The open space on which the fair was built was turned into St. Louis's famed Forest Park. ■

The Short-Lived Peace

The Louisiana Purchase Exposition left Missouri eager to expand. People were just investigating ways to do that when the United States entered World War I against Germany in 1917. More than 150,000 Missourians joined the armed forces. General John J. ("Black Jack") Pershing, who grew up in Laclede, Missouri, led U.S. troops to France, where they fought bravely in the trenches. Missouri casualties totaled 11,172, making up one-fifth of the 53,407 Americans killed in that war.

On the home front, Missourians rallied to the nation's call for help. They bought war bonds to help finance the cause. Almost 1,500 Missouri doctors closed their offices and offered their services. Women sewed hospital gowns, worked for the

St. Louis's Louisiana Purchase Exposition

A Victory Bond drive during World War I

Dogged Courage

Wrinkles was the pet of Sergeant Archie Boyd of Grant City, a sniper serving in the U.S. Army in France. The little dog was wounded by shrapnel three times but continued to carry messages between Boyd and his commanding officer. At the end of the war, the governments of both France and Italy decorated Wrinkles for his bravery. ■

Red Cross, and planted "thrift gardens." When the servicemen and women returned, they were greeted with parades, praise, and—most important—jobs.

Zeal for Reform

Soldiers returning home were met by a mood of reform, especially for banning the manufacture and sale of alcoholic beverages. Called the temperance movement, the idea had long been popular in Missouri. Among the leaders of the antisaloon forces in the 1890s was Carry Nation, famed for smashing the interiors of taverns with a hatchet. She lived for a time in the towns of Holden and Belton, Missouri.

Carry Nation didn't live to see it, but in 1919, Missouri supported passage of the Eighteenth Amendment to the U.S. Constitution. This amendment prohibited the sale of alcohol. Prohibition, nicknamed the Noble Experiment, was the law of the land for the next fourteen years.

Many Missourians objected to restrictions on their drinking and went to great lengths to get a beer or a drink of whiskey. Gangsters, drawn by the promise of quick money, moved in to supply the demand by bringing in liquor from Canada or Mexico. The Cuckoos, the Bergers, and Egan's Rats were among the gangs that waged bloody battles over their criminal turf in St. Louis, Kansas City, and other Missouri communities. Law-abiding citizens who saw their cities controlled by gangsters were relieved when Prohibition was repealed in 1933, and they could take back their state.

Carry Nation

Chapter Four

In the National Limelight

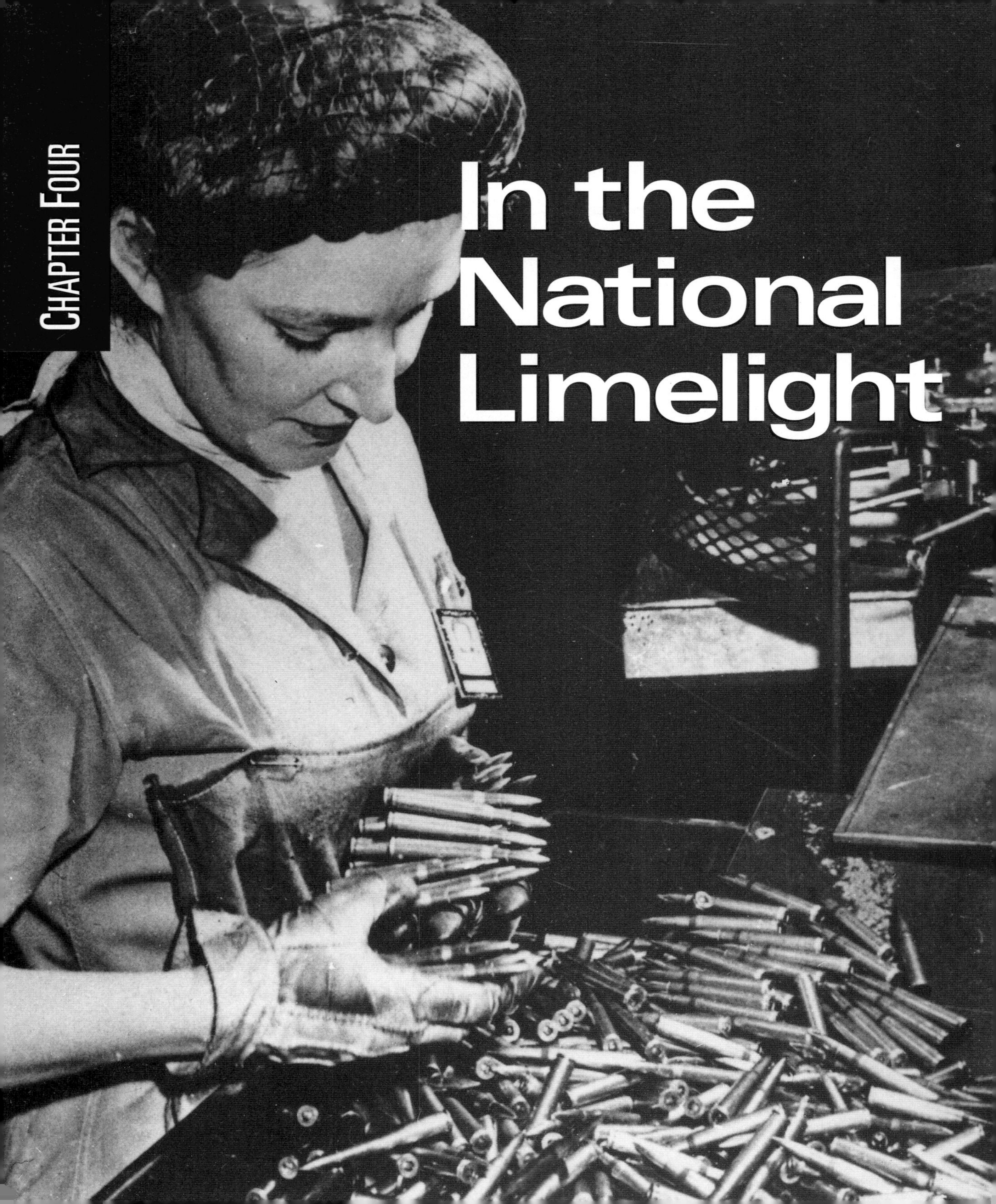

Missouri traditionally voted for Democratic candidates for public office. But many Missourians blamed President Woodrow Wilson, a Democrat, for getting the nation into World War I. They also objected to his dream for a League of Nations, which was to be an international peacekeeping body like today's United Nations. Many Missourians were isolationists. They wanted to keep the United States out of other countries' affairs. Missouri senator James A. Reed was instrumental in preventing the United States from joining the League of Nations, despite Wilson's certainty that such an organization could not survive without the United States.

Woodrow Wilson promoting the League of Nations

Adding to the Democrats' dilemma, consumer prices rose and farm prices dropped. People were worried about paying their bills. When the Republicans promised better times, Missourians helped sweep them into office on both the national and the state level.

A Republican Era

Arthur M. Hyde was the first of three Republican governors elected in Missouri in the 1920s. A former car dealer, he was a Progressive Republican who wanted to link all parts of the state by an improved transportation system. Missouri residents were trading in their

Opposite: Readying bullet cartridges for testing in World War II

Men paving Highway 24 in the 1920s

horses and buggies for cars, so paved roads were urgently needed. He established a state highway system and set up a highway commissioner to supervise its construction. Hyde also called a constitutional convention to update the state's primary legal document, and he established the state park system.

Sam A. Baker, a former state superintendent of schools, was the next Republican governor. He pushed a worker's compensation program through the General Assembly to provide financial protection for workers injured on the job. In 1928, Baker was considered as a Republican candidate for vice president of the United States, but he lost the nomination.

Henry S. Caulfield, governor of Missouri

The Great Depression

The third Republican governor of the era, Henry S. Caulfield, led the state through the unhappy depths of the Great Depression. Following the stock market crash in 1929, this worldwide economic collapse prevented him from initiating many new programs. But he succeeded in setting up a state welfare system for the neediest citizens. Tens of thousands of desperate Missourians had lost their jobs, their farms, and their life's savings, so Caulfield's economic aid kept many families together.

It took a Democratic president—Franklin D. Roosevelt—and a program called the New Deal to pull the United States, and Missouri, out of its economic misery. Roosevelt created many federal

Lucky Lindy Flies Solo

Charles A. Lindbergh (1902–1974) became a hero in 1927 and put St. Louis on the map for his solo nonstop flight across the Atlantic Ocean—the first ever made. Lindbergh had been an airmail pilot, flying from St. Louis to Chicago. When a prize for the first nonstop solo flight from New York to Paris was offered, Lindbergh persuaded St. Louis businessmen to sponsor him. In return, he named his tiny plane *Spirit of St. Louis*.

On May 20, 1927, Lindbergh took off from a field on Long Island in New York. Every inch of space in the plane was filled with tanks of gasoline. The 3,600-mile (5,793-km) flight took him thirty-three hours and thirty minutes. On his lonely, starlit way, he had only five sandwiches to eat and two canteens of water. *Spirit of St. Louis* is now on display at the National Air and Space Museum in Washington, D.C. ■

Tune In to Radio

In 1921, WEW, the first radio station in Missouri, began broadcasting at St. Louis University. The next year, a station was established at Jefferson City. The programs on these first stations consisted only of music and market reports. In 1923, a speech delivered in St. Louis by President Warren G. Harding marked the first time Missourians heard a political address by radio. ■

programs to help people recover economically. Some congressional representatives opposed the federal government's involvement in so many parts of people's lives. Senator Harry S. Truman, a democrat from Independence who had been elected in 1935, helped Roosevelt push through his reforms.

Another Terrible War

Ironically, the misery of the Great Depression was halted by the misery of World War II. In 1941, the Japanese bombed Pearl Harbor in Hawaii, and the United States joined the nations fighting the Axis, or Germany, Japan, and Italy. Over the next four years, more than 450,000 men and women from Missouri served in the military.

Riveters working on an airplane

One of the United States' most brilliant generals, Omar Bradley, was a native of Clark, Missouri. He led the U.S. troops during the D-Day invasion of Europe in June 1944, when Britain, the United States, and other Allied forces landed in Europe, determined to put an end to Axis aggression.

One more time, the hometown folks helped out. The state's industrial muscle was flexed as thousands of extra workers, including women, were hired to replace men who went to the battlefront. Kansas City's North American Aviation made bombers. The Kaw Point shipyards on the Missouri River turned out landing craft. Children collected scrap metal, bottles, and papers for recycling. Victory Gardens were planted in backyards so that farm-fresh vegetables could be shipped to the armed forces around the world.

The Missouri President

In 1944, President Roosevelt asked Truman to be his vice presidential candidate for his fourth run at the presidency. The native of Lamar who had lived most of his life in Independence became the vice president of the United States.

The quiet Missourian had served in that position less than three months, however, when Roosevelt died. Truman quickly took over the reins of government as president, but soon found himself faced with a terrible decision.

In 1945, wanting to end the war with the least number of Allied casualties, Truman reluctantly ordered atomic bombs to be dropped on civilian targets in Japan. After the fighting ended,

Whoops! Spoke Too Soon

Truman was elected as president for his own full term in 1948, despite a close vote. The race was so tight that the *Chicago Daily Tribune* printed a front-page story saying that Truman's Republican opponent, Thomas E. Dewey, had won! Some copies of the paper were distributed before all the votes were counted and it turned out that Truman had won. ■

his Truman Doctrine was instrumental in rebuilding war-shattered nations. In addition, he helped form the new United Nations (U.N.).

Truman had barely settled into his own term in office when communist North Korea invaded South Korea. The president's swift military response saved South Korea from being overrun in 1950. But then he had another very tough decision. General Douglas MacArthur, hero of the Pacific Campaign in World War II and commander of the U.N. forces in Korea, was immensely popular with the public. MacArthur wanted to invade China, one of North Korea's allies, but Truman blocked the move. The general made his objections public, so Truman relieved him of his command for not supporting the policy of the United States and U.N. Many people around the country never forgave Truman for firing MacArthur.

Truman did not run for another term. He retired to his home in Independence, where he worked on his papers and supervised his presidential library. He died there in 1972.

The Swinging Voters

Missouri supported winning Republican presidential candidate Dwight D. Eisenhower in 1952 but switched to Democrat Adlai Stevenson of neighboring Illinois in 1956. Stevenson lost the election, the first time since 1904 that Missouri had not backed a victorious presidential candidate.

Democrat James T. Blair Jr., a war hero and a longtime Missouri political figure, was elected governor in 1956, but he and his wife refused to move into the governor's mansion because it badly needed repairs. Missourians sang a funny song about the situation:

This old house is full of spiders
This old house is full of rats,
The old house ain't fit for entertaining
Good old Democrats.

This old mansion is in tatters
This old place needs lots of work
If I'd known it last November,
I'd have run for county clerk.

Governor and Mrs. James Blair Jr. looking at the worn carpet of the governor's mansion

On the national level, Missouri Democrats did better in 1960. They supported John F. Kennedy against his Republican rival, Richard Nixon. Senator Stuart Symington of Missouri made a bid for the presidency in that year as a "favorite son" candidate with the Democrats, but did not get the nomination.

The youngest Missouri governor in fifty-six years was Warren E. Hearnes, who took the oath of office in 1965. Although he was only forty-one at the time, Hearnes was well known in Missouri thanks to his previous job as secretary of state. During his term, the state's General Assembly passed a bill outlawing racial discrimination in public places. It also set up training centers for the mentally challenged and established state-supported colleges in Joplin and St. Joseph.

Christopher S. Bond

Elected in 1972, Christopher S. Bond was truly the youngest Missouri governor—only thirty-three when he took office. He was also the first Republican governor in twenty-eight years. Bond helped reorganize the state's executive branch, making 45,000 state employees responsible to seven commission directors who

Tallest Building Designed by Sullivan

In 1973, the state purchased the ten-story Wainwright Building in St. Louis, considered to be the first U.S. skyscraper. Built about 1890 by famed Chicago architect Louis Sullivan, it was Sullivan's only skyscraper and the earliest attempt to make a skyscraper design different from smaller buildings. The state of Missouri turned the landmark building into state offices.

then reported directly to the governor. It was the first serious reshuffling of the executive department in the state's history.

The Troubled '70s and '80s

The 1970s and early 1980s were troubled times for Missouri. The state faced environmental, social, and economic challenges. A massive flood in 1973 covered 1.8 million acres (729,000 ha) of land and caused

Missouri workers helping pump water during the 1973 flood

An Example of Progress

In 1980, Dr. James Frank was elected president of the National Collegiate Athletic Association (NCAA), the organization that oversees athletics between colleges. As president of Lincoln University in Jefferson City, Frank had led a national effort to integrate athletic programs for women into the NCAA. He was one of numerous black Missourians who were now becoming national figures in many fields. From business to education, minorities became better recognized for their talent and creativity. ■

millions of dollars in damage. Concerned state voters put a cap, or limit, on spending by state government, which severely affected how Missouri could take care of its less fortunate citizens. The governor subsequently froze salaries of state workers until the budget spending situation was resolved.

In this troubled era, several large companies pulled out of the state and relocated elsewhere. In response, Missouri launched a massive marketing campaign promoting the state as good for business. In 1977, Missouri opened an office in

First Woman Elected

In 1984, Harriet Woods was elected Missouri's lieutenant governor, the first woman ever elected to that office in the state. She had previously served eight years as a state senator. After her term was over, she moved onto the national scene and became president of the National Women's Political Caucus. ■

The Middle of the Country

The population center of the United States moved into Missouri from Illinois after the census of 1980. Across the United States, there are an equal number of people living in any direction outward from the population center. In 1980, that point was DeSoto in Jefferson County. After the 1990 census, it moved to 9.7 miles (15.6 km) northwest of Steelville in Crawford County. As the West and Southwest grow, the nation's population center will continue to move westward. ■

Düsseldorf, Germany, to seek foreign investment. As a result, a number of new firms moved in to replace those that had left. Slowly, the state experienced an economic turnaround. By 1989, prosperity was obviously creeping back. Workers were rehired, farm prices were up. Life was better.

Into the Twenty-First Century

As Missourians look to the future they will have to contend with many hard issues. Under able and strong leaders who are carrying the state into the next century, Missourians work diligently to maintain the state as a great place in which to live. There are 170 public libraries and 70 college and university libraries, as well as numerous excellent city and county library systems. Bookmobiles trundle throughout the state, opening new creative windows to citizens in outlying areas.

Scientific and technological education is promoted throughout the state's universities. Both Columbia and Rolla have centers for

Governor Mel Carnahan

nuclear studies. Missouri and its neighboring states formed development groups to promote business throughout their entire area. The arts flourish. The "can-do" spirit of Missourians is the reason why the state continues to do well.

Chapter Five

The Neighborly State

The Mississippi River as seen from the bluffs in Hannibal

Missouri is neighborly. It has more states as neighbors than any state except Tennessee. Tucked away in the Midwestern United States, Missouri has Iowa on the north; Illinois, Kentucky, and Tennessee on the east; Arkansas on the south; and Nebraska, Kansas, and Oklahoma on the west.

The total land area of the state equals 69,709 square miles (180,546 sq km). It is the twenty-first-largest state in the United States and is larger than every state east of the Mississippi River.

A Joining of Geographic Areas

Four major geographic areas unite to form the state of Missouri. These areas are the glaciated plains of the northwest, the western plains, the Ozark Mountains of the south, and the southeastern lowlands.

The "Mighty Mo"—the Missouri River—begins in the Rocky Mountains and flows southeastward, finally giving its name to the state before emptying into the Mississippi River. The Missouri River cuts into the state at Kansas City and then crosses the middle of the state to St. Louis. The river drains most of Missouri,

Opposite: The Ozark Mountains

helped by the waters of the Platte, Grand, Nodaway, and other rivers that flow into it. To the north of the mighty Missouri are rolling hills, plains, and prairies stretching north to Iowa.

South of the Missouri River lies land untouched by ancient glaciers. This land is rugged, with sheer cliffs, deep valleys, and rocky ridges. Clear, cold springs bubble from the recesses of mysterious caves, while waterfalls plunge down the hillsides. Trout-filled streams meander through thick oak forests. Near Missouri's western border, the elevation reaches 850 feet (259 m) above sea level.

The Land of Caves

Leasburg, a village in Crawford County, was founded in 1859 and named after Samuel Lea, the area's first settler. On the nearby Lost River is Onondaga Cave, which tourists can enter in flat-bottomed boats. The boats travel into the cave for about 900 feet (274 m), carrying explorers to a landing where gravel paths lead off into the darkness. Numerous types of onyx rock are found in there.

Onondaga Cave

Quaking Missouri

It might be a surprise that Missouri's southeastern lowlands have been regularly jarred by earthquakes. Three of the greatest earthquakes in the United States occurred here during 1811 and 1812. They measured 8.4 to 8.7 on the Richter scale, which is a mechanical way of measuring the force of a quake. (The San Francisco earthquake of 1906 was probably less than 8.3.) Even as far away as Boston, Detroit, and Washington, D.C., sidewalks split and the upper stories of buildings crumbled in these quakes.

The quake that occurred on December 16, 1811, altered the Mississippi River channel near New Madrid and created deep new lakes. Vast sections of land submerged, while others rose higher. Steamboats were tossed up on land like toys.

No deaths were recorded, but a similar quake today would devastate this more populated part of Missouri. Earthquakes are still felt occasionally in the area. Sometimes, even St. Louis is shaken. The region recorded major shocks in 1967 and 1975. Geologists think that another big quake will occur in the New Madrid area someday, but nobody knows exactly when. ■

Other caves in the region are part of a huge system of caves that are formed in limestone. Many of these caves have fallen in, sometimes leaving arches of harder rock seen as natural bridges. Some caves are show caverns, where visitors can see stalactites and stalagmites. Marvel Cave at Branson is the third-largest show cave in the United States. Other spectacular caverns include Crystal Cave near Cassville, Ozark Caverns in Lake of the Ozarks, and Fantasy World Caverns at Eldon. Missouri has so many caves—there may be 5,000—that it is sometimes called the Cave State.

The Mississippi River rolls along Missouri's eastern side. The southeastern part of the state, the Boot Heel, is part of the alluvial plain of the Mississippi Valley, formed where the river deposited its silt along the bank. The elevation of this plain is less than 500 feet (152 m). Before it was artificially drained around the year 1900, this region was swampy. The standing water was the home of beaver, muskrat, and waterbirds, but they stood in the way of development. When drained, this fertile area became some of the most valuable farming land in Missouri.

Mountain, Parks, and Forests

The Ozark Plateau is actually a line of eroded mountaintops north of the southeast lowlands. They stretch north of the Missouri River in the east. The highest point in the state is Taum Sauk Mountain at 1,772 feet (540 m), near Glover. The average elevation in this area is 1,000 to 1,400 feet (305 m to 427 m) above sea level.

Missouri's parks and forests

Because the area is too rocky and rough to be farmed, most of the state's hardwood forests are situated on the Ozark hills. Today, only one-third of Missouri remains forested, compared with two-thirds before the Europeans arrived. Oak, maple, walnut, birch, and pine are the most common of the state's 140 species of trees. Thirty-seven species make up 90 percent of the trees throughout the state.

The Mark Twain National Forest covers 1.5 million acres (607,287 ha), with eight sections in the Ozarks and another east of Columbia. The forest provides a perfect getaway for hunters, fishing fans, campers, hikers, and off-road cyclists.

Restoration projects at thirty state parks are designed to bring back the state's landscapes and the biological diversity that was originally so important to the environment. Sometimes, grassy areas are carefully burned to restore prairies and savannas. Among the state parks being restored are Ha Ha Tonka in the Upper Ozarks, Prairie in southwestern prairie, Roaring River in the White River region, Hawn in southeastern Missouri, Pershing in northern Missouri, and Big Oak Tree in the Boot Heel district.

All Missourians are encouraged to visit the parks and forests. For instance, Braille signs and paved walkways at Elephant Rocks State Park and other sites help those with physical challenges. In addition, many

Mark Twain National Forest

young people join the state's junior naturalist program. They learn to identify trees and animals, and help pick up litter and repair trails.

Missouri is making certain that land damaged by mining is reclaimed. This Reclamation for Recreation program assures state residents that mining companies will clean up their mined areas so that the land can be reused for recreational purposes.

Finger Lakes State Park was created in the 1960s after a coal-mining company strip-mined (tore away the surface of) the area in the central part of the state. The damaged landscape was filled with water and stocked with fish.

Elephant Rocks State Park

A Very Long, Very Narrow State Park

The rails may be going, but the hikers are coming. The Katy Trail, which is being built across the state along the route of an old railroad, lures hikers and bikers from around the country. Managed by the Missouri Department of Natural Resources, the trail (and its state park) will eventually be more than 250 miles (400 km) long, the longest such rail-to-trail conversion in the nation. By the late 1990s, it already covered 186 miles (299 km) from St. Charles to Sedalia. The Missouri River parallels much of the right-of-way, with many historic towns along the way. The trail gets its name from the old Missouri-Kansas-Texas (MKT) Railroad.

Pleasure Afloat

Located in southeast Missouri around the Current and Jacks Fork Rivers, the Ozark National Scenic Riverways, headquartered at Van Buren, include more than 134 miles (216 km) of spring-fed streams and hundreds of caves. The federal protection of these scenic areas started in the 1920s.

The rivers and creeks making up the scenic waterways, called float streams, are fed by fast-moving water from underground springs. They can be traveled on rafts or paddled in canoes, with varying degrees of difficulty. These waterways pass through beautiful wilderness and challenge fishing fans.

Missouri has a number of artificial waterways. Built to provide hydroelectric power and prevent flooding, the lakes are also great places for recreation. The huge Lake of the Ozarks was created by damming the Osage River. It spreads over almost 60,000 acres (24,300 ha), with a convoluted shoreline 1,375 miles (2,213 km) long. It is one of the largest artificial lakes in the United States, reaching across the counties of Camden, Miller, Morgan, Benton, Henry, and St. Clair. On the western end of the lake, the Harry S. Truman Reservoir adds to the attractions.

Dedicated fishing vacationers kick back on the lake while waiting for black bass, silver bass, crappie, walleyed pike,

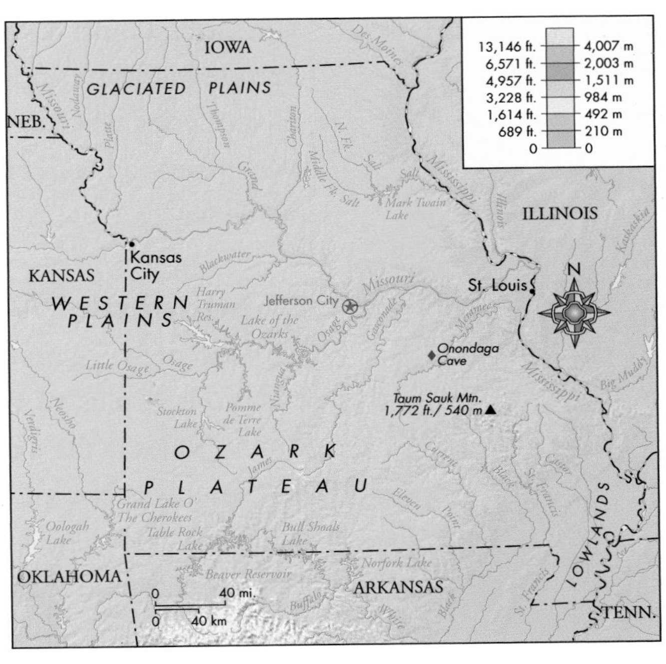

Missouri's topography

Smoke tree in bloom

and perch to bite. In summer, the surrounding forest captures the eye with its colorful sumac, sassafras, and other foliage. The autumn trees explode with brilliant colors of crimson, orange, and yellow.

Missouri has more than 400,000 acres (161,943 ha) of glades—stretches of very dry land covered with thin soil suitable only for grazing cattle. The open hillsides are covered with limestone, dolomite, chert, sandstone, and shale. Plants such as the smoke tree, purple beard-tongue, and Ashe's juniper have adapted to the desertlike terrain. Some push taproots into the cracks of rock, while others thrive only during winter and spring when the water supply is abundant. White-tailed deer, wild turkeys, and most other animals pass through the glades on their search for food.

Changeable Weather

Because of its central location, Missouri gets weather from all directions. Bouts of cold air whistle down through the central United States in the winter. Warm air from the Gulf of Mexico and dry southwestern air balance that in the spring, summer, and autumn. Missourians joke that they can never accurately predict the weather because it changes so quickly.

Missouri's Geographical Features

Total area; rank	69,709 sq. mi. (180,546 sq km); 21st
Land; rank	68,896 sq. mi. (178,441 sq km); 18th
Water; rank	811 sq. mi. (2,100 sq km); 32nd
***Inland water*; rank**	811 sq. mi. (2,100 sq km); 26th
Geographic center	Miller, 20 miles (32 km) southwest of Jefferson City
Highest point	Taum Sauk Mountain, 1,772 feet (540 m)
Lowest point	St. Francis River, 230 feet (70 m)
Largest city	Kansas City
Population; rank	5,137,804 (1990 census); 15th
Record high temperature	118°F (48°C) at Clinton on July 15, 1936, at Lamar on July 18, 1936, and at Warsaw and Union on July 14, 1954
Record low temperature	–40°F (–40°C) at Warsaw on February 13, 1905
Average July temperature	78°F (26°C)
Average January temperature	30°F (–1°C)
Average annual precipitation	40 inches (102 cm)

Missouri summers are generally long, warm, and humid, while winters are fairly brisk and invigorating. Temperatures range from below 0°F (–17°C) to 100°F (37.8°C). The temperature in January averages 30°F (–1°C); in the summer it averages 78°F (26°C).

Rainfall, a third of it occurring between April and June, varies between 34 inches (86.4 cm) and more than 50 inches (127 cm). One of the most amazing rainfalls occurred at Holt on June 22, 1947, when 12 inches (31 cm) of rain fell in 42 minutes, making a world's record.

Missouri's rainfall is generally adequate to support the state's crops. Its rainfall and its natural drainage system make Missouri's soil ideal for farming in both the northern and southern regions. The combination of rain, soils, and temperature allows a growing season ranging from 210 days in the south to 170 days in the north.

Heavy snow is unusual for the state, but some snow falls between December and February. Missouri also rests in what the U.S. Weather Service calls "Tornado Alley." Missouri has an average of twenty-seven dangerous twisters every year.

Living Countryside

Wild animals were once plentiful in Missouri. Larger animals, including elk, bison, black bear, and deer, roamed the prairies and forests. Turkeys, beaver, otters, and mink also made the state their home. But human settlement destroyed many of the habitats of the larger mammals. In addition, trapping and the fur trade were profitable businesses for the area's first settlers, leading to the

Tornado damage to a grain-storage bin

National Wildlife Refuges

There are four National Wildlife Refuges in Missouri. They all feature the great fishing and bird-watching that is found at Clarence Cannon. Even larger, though, is Mingo, in the east, which incorporates swampland created by the shifting Mississippi River. Swan Lake protects migrating Canada geese. Squaw Creek is home to several hundred bald eagles.

near-extinction of some mammals. While most of these animals have diminished in number or have left Missouri entirely, the deer population has risen dramatically over the last forty years.

Colorful Countryside

Missouri is a bird-watchers' paradise. Robins, bluebirds, meadowlarks, cardinals, orioles, hawks, owls, quail, doves, and thrushes fill the skies. Their feathers are often as bright as the wildflowers dancing through the woodlands and parks.

The first blossoms in the spring are dogtooth violet, toothwort, Dutchman's breeches, and mayapples. Later in the season, wild ginger, wake robin, bloodroot, and jack-in-the-pulpit decorate wooded slopes. Roadsides, prairies, and glades are graced with Indian paintbrush, wild hyacinth, blue-eyed grass, and wood betony. The Ozark Plateau's bluffs and valleys have plants like the royal catchfly, fringed poppy mallow, and gayfeather. Bluegrass, although not native to Missouri, is also plentiful.

The only poisonous snakes in Missouri are the rattlesnake and the copperhead. Since they keep to themselves, they are generally not a problem for people.

Jefferson City during the Great Flood of 1993

The Appeal and Danger of Water

Throughout history, people have settled near rivers and lakes where fertile soil, water transportation, fresh drinking water, and other natural benefits are provided. However, there are risks to living near rivers. Floods on its rivers—big and small—have plagued Missouri over the years. In May 1892, the Big Piney River rose 30 feet (9 m) in eight hours after a ferocious thunderstorm. In 1951, a tremendous flood devastated the Missouri River region, wiping out the packing industry in Kansas City. And in 1973, millions of acres of land was destroyed in a flood.

But few floods have been as devastating as the Great Flood of 1993. An unusual amount of rainy weather had saturated the soil for several months before the actual flooding, which started in the spring and continued off and on through November. When it was over, 112 of the state's counties had been declared disaster areas. Forty-nine people died, and damage to land and property was estimated at $4 billion. Coffins were washed out of cemeteries. Huge gas-storage tanks burned after being hit by floating debris. Hundreds of homes and businesses were ruined.

Although the destruction was widespread, Missourians learned about the kindness of their neighbors—and the importance of preparing for future floods. Extra shelters and first-aid stations were built around the state, levees, or dikes, were raised and strengthened, and construction of buildings was prohibited on some floodplains.

Missouri is now ready to face whatever Mother Nature tosses its way.

Chapter Six

A Rich Diversity of Towns

Missouri has dozens of delightful cities and villages. All are rich in history, and all are quite different. Those on the east seem like cities of the East. Those on the west are right at home with cattle and horses.

The fence-painting competition during Hannibal's Tom Sawyer Days

The Road Through the North

U.S. Highway 36 links several interesting towns across northern Missouri. From Hannibal on the east to St. Joseph on the west, the highway cuts straight through rich farm country and rolling forestland. Along the way are Long Branch and Pershing State Parks, Swan Lake National Wildlife Refuge, and the Fountain Grove Wildlife Area.

Hannibal is famed for author Mark Twain. Kids love coming to Hannibal to recreate the fence-painting scene from Mark Twain's great novel, *Tom Sawyer*. A national fence-painting competition is held each July at the National Tom Sawyer Days festival.

Twain, whose real name was Samuel Langhorne Clemens, grew up in Hannibal. This was a typical river town, catering, like St. Louis, its neighbor 117 miles (188 km) to the south, to the riverboat trade. Tourism is now Hannibal's major industry, with visitors exploring all the sites from Twain's life. The Mark Twain Cave is

Opposite: A view of the University of Missouri campus in Columbia

Ex-Governor Becomes Confederate General

Confederate general Sterling Price was a native of Keytesville, the seat of north-central Missouri's Chariton County. A bronze statue of General Price stands in the city square. Born in Virginia, he moved to Missouri in 1831. Price was elected to Congress in 1844 but resigned to fight in the Mexican War (1846–1848). During that conflict, he rose to the rank of major general. In 1852, Price was elected governor of Missouri. When the Civil War broke out in 1861, he joined the army again, but this time it was the army of the Confederacy—the South.

Price fought in many Civil War battles and finally was defeated at Westport in October 1864. This was the conflict's last campaign in Missouri. When the war ended with the defeat of the Confederacy, he refused to surrender to the Union forces. The general fled to Mexico, where he tried to start a colony for ex-Confederate soldiers. But when the Mexican emperor, who had supported the idea, was overthrown, the colony collapsed. Price returned to St. Louis in 1866, where he later died. ■

fun to explore, and the Becky Thatcher home, where Tom's friend Becky supposedly lived, is a page from the past. Hannibal's Mark Twain Bridge across the Mississippi was completed in 1935.

Heading west, Highway 36 comes to Marceline, the boyhood home of Walt Disney. Kids can even sit at the famed movie executive's school desk. Disney premiered his Civil War movie, *The Great Locomotive Chase*, in the city's Uptown Theater in 1956. Marceline's main street supposedly was the model for the Main Street in California's Disneyland.

Ponies and Bank Robbers

April 3 is an important date for the residents of St. Joseph, on Missouri's far western border. On April 3, 1860, the Pony Express began its mail service to outposts in the far West. On April 3, 1882, bank robber Jesse James was shot and killed in a house there. The town's Pony Express National Memorial and the Jesse James Home Museum bring those days back to life.

The Pony Express

Just as the Civil War was about to start, an effort to pull the United States together with quick communications began in St. Joseph. The boys of the Pony Express carried mail from St. Joseph to Sacramento, California, changing horses every few miles so that they could cross the country in about ten days.

The enterprise lasted only eighteen months and was put out of business by the completion of the transcontinental telegraph. But it went down in history as one of the United States' great romantic endeavors.

Beauty and Beef

To the south of St. Joseph is Kansas City, the state's largest city, which one Missouri poet called "a city built on bread and beef." The town grew up where the Kansas (also called the Kaw) and Missouri Rivers meet. With a population of 435,146 in 1990 and about 1.5 million in the metropolitan area, the city is the thirty-first largest city in the United States.

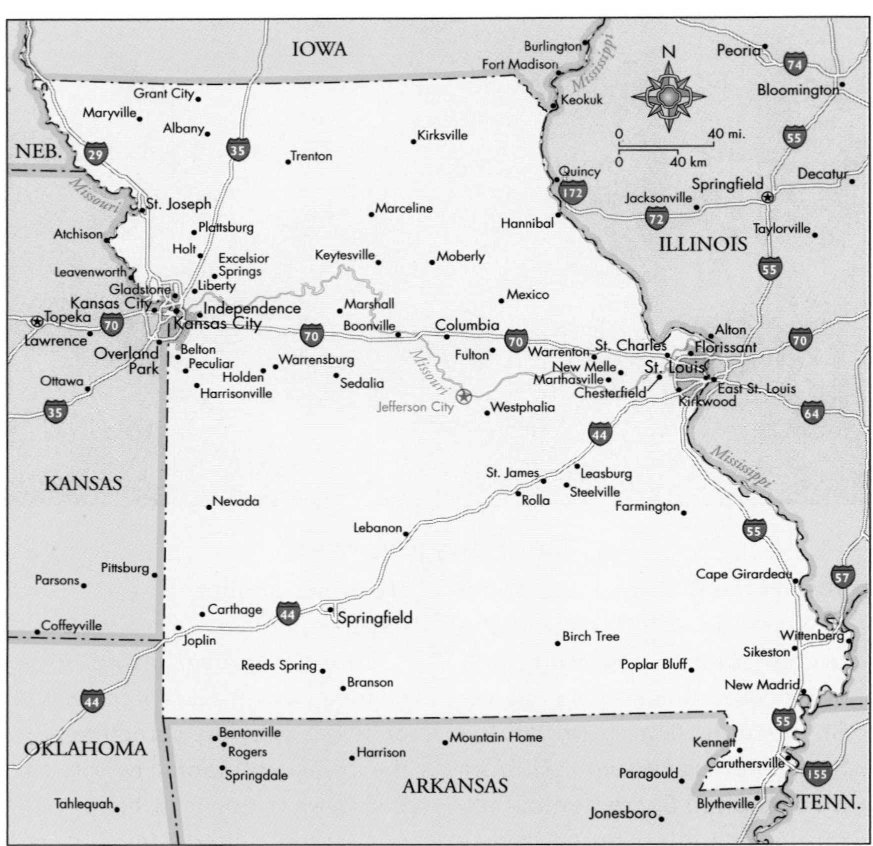

Missouri's cities and interstates

Kansas City is in the United States' agricultural heartland. About 78 percent of the nation's wheat, 80 percent of its cattle, 90 percent of its corn, 89 percent of its soybeans, and 89 percent of its hogs, are grown almost within sight of downtown Kansas City. Its much smaller neighbor—Kansas City, Kansas—is just across the state border.

Kansas City began as two communities. One was called Kansas and the other was Westport. The town of Kansas, which grew around a fur-trading post in the early 1820s, has long since disappeared. But Westport was incorporated in 1833 as a cattle-punching town full of cowboys, and later became the site of Missouri's last Civil War battle. Westport, now a trendy neighborhood of restaurants and shops, and Kansas merged as Kansas City in 1899.

As the center of the U.S. cattle industry moved west, the stockyards where the cattle were slaughtered moved too. From Chicago, they went to Kansas City, which is when the city acquired its reputation for fine beef. Today, the stockyards and feeding lots have moved to Colorado, but Kansas City has found new ways of thriving.

Kansas City today is an industrial center. Its companies produce automobiles, farm equipment, frozen foods, greeting cards, clothing and chemicals. Some familiar items were invented by Kansas City researchers. Among them were Teflon, a coating for kitchen utensils, an ice cream dessert called Eskimo Pie, and M&M candy.

The wild animals at the Kansas City Zoo range from lions, bears, and tigers to exotic pygmy marmosets, red kangaroos, and lesser pandas. This excellent zoo has more than 600 creatures.

Tamer animals, too, are found in Kansas City. The American Royal, which started in 1899, is the largest combined livestock, horse show, and rodeo in the United States. For two weeks each autumn, the show brings together nearly 2,000 horses and 4,000 head of cattle, hogs, and sheep from around the United States and Canada.

Present-day Westport

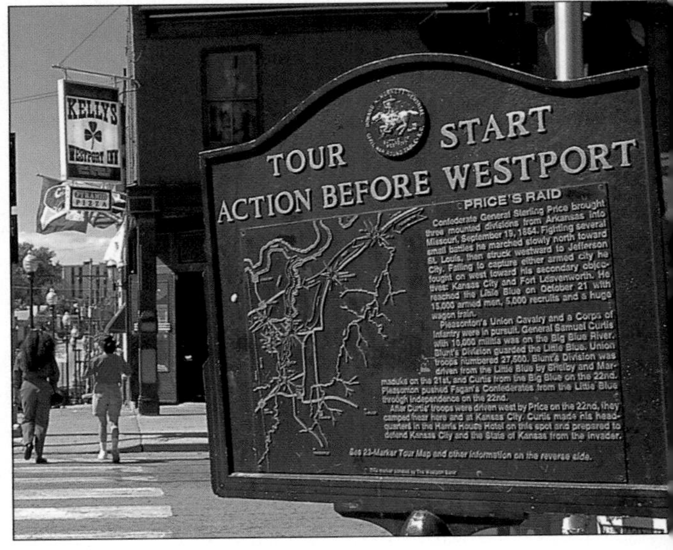

Kansas City's Caves

Missouri is sometimes called the Cave State. And many of its huge caves lie underneath Kansas City. For decades, these caves have been a benefit to Kansas City business. The walls are painted, and there are roads running through them, creating a whole second level to the city. They are sometimes used as offices and sometimes as storage areas for perishable items, which are well preserved in the unchanging temperature deep underground. ■

The Dream Community

J. C. Nichols purchased land south of Kansas City in 1907. Although the land was a rubbish pit for the stockyards at that time, Nichols envisioned a dream community for people willing to pay top dollar to live there. He set to work building what he called a "quality" suburb, with winding roads, parks, statues, and fountains. The Country Club District, as he called it, was one of the United States' first planned communities. ■

Since the 1920s, the Future Farmers of America has held its national convention in conjunction with the show. More than 22,000 farm kids from all over the country flock to learn techniques of showing their own animals at hometown fairs.

After a trip to Spain in the 1920s, land developer J. C. Nichols, who built up parts of Kansas City in the early 1900s, returned to Kansas City and built Country Club Plaza, the country's first shopping center. The plaza's Spanish architecture and wide boulevards were the talk of the nation. Eventually, the expanding city surrounded the Country Club

District. Today, the neighborhood remains one of the most exclusive in Kansas City.

Kansas City brags that it has more fountains than any city except Rome, Italy, and more miles of boulevards, or landscaped streets, than Paris, France. Its downtown Crown Center includes hotels, performance spaces, and plenty of great places for skateboarders. The city's massive Liberty Memorial honors the men and women who served in World War I.

Not So Independent

The city of Independence was originally 5 miles (8 km) east of Kansas City and separated by countryside, but now the cities abut one another. Independence has long been noted in the history

One of Kansas City's fountains

Finger-Licking Barbecue

Kansas City is hailed as the "Barbecue Capital of the World." Beginning in the 1920s, a man named Henry Perry made Kansas City famous by barbecuing its great beef over an outdoor pit and wrapping the cooked slabs of juicy meat in newspaper. Today, Kansas Citians barbecue just about everything from turkey to shrimp, as well as the traditional beef and pork.

Chopped onion, tomatoes, celery, white vinegar, chili powder, Worcestershire sauce, Tabasco sauce, green pepper, and other ingredients make up sauces for a finger-licking, napkin-friendly meal. There are many competitions to see who makes the best barbecue. Kansas City author Shifra Stein has written several award-winning cookbooks highlighting the city's barbecuing achievements.

books for its importance as beginning for Western settlement. In 1846, the first stage coaches rolled out of Independence on their way to Santa Fe, New Mexico. As the starting point for the Oregon, California, and Santa Fe Trails, on which traders and settlers went west, Independence is commemorated in the National Frontier Trails Center.

On a more modern note, the library housing the official papers of President Harry S. Truman is a popular spot for scholars. It was dedicated in 1957. The president's home is on a tree-lined street nearby. Neighbors still remember Truman and his wife, Bess, in their later years, going for walks around the block.

Kansas City–Style Barbecue Sauce

Ingredients:

3 cups beef stock or canned broth
1/4 cup white vinegar
1/2 cup Worcestershire sauce
1 cup tomato paste
1/2 cup brown sugar
1/2 cup white sugar
1 tbl. chili powder
2 tbl. liquid smoke
1/3 cup mustard
1 tsp. cayenne pepper or hot sauce
2 garlic cloves, chopped

Directions:

Mix all ingredients together in a large saucepan. Cook over medium heat for 25 minutes, stirring constantly. Lower heat and simmer for another 40 minutes to 1 hour. The sauce should be thick and smooth, but should not be allowed to burn or dry out.

This sauce can be served with almost any meat. Try beef ribs, pork shoulder, brisket, chicken, or anything you like.

The Missouri Capital

The official name of Jefferson City, or Jeff City as the locals call it, is the City of Jefferson. It was selected as Missouri's capital on December 31, 1821. Located on the Missouri River in the center of the state, 108 miles (174 km) west of St. Louis, the site seems geographically perfect. But the town got off to a shaky start. Only a tavern and mission church stood at Jefferson when it was named as the state's chief city. However, the hometown folks were optimistic. They improved the roads, penned their hogs, and laid out building sites in a plan designed by Daniel Boone's son. The original statehouse was built

The International Spotlight

In March 1999, newsmakers from around the world came to the Truman Library at Independence to watch three former communist nations become members of the North Atlantic Treaty Organization (NATO). Truman helped found NATO after World War II to unite the nations that were determined to oppose the Soviet Union's domination of other nations. After the Soviet Union collapsed in the early 1990s and official communism ended, the Czech Republic, Hungary, and Poland were quick to turn against communism and asked to become members of NATO. A new era in world history had begun.

in 1822 at the location of the governor's mansion today. The building cost only $18,573 to construct.

The first permanent capitol burned in 1837 and was replaced by another building. That also was destroyed by fire, in 1911. Today's statehouse was completed in 1917 on the south shore of the Missouri River. Jefferson City is quite small for a state capital with fewer than 40,000 residents, but it is the home of Lincoln University.

Jefferson City's capitol

Just north of Jefferson City stands Columbia, a city built for education. It is the home of the University of Missouri, nicknamed "Mizzou" by its students. In 1822, the Boone's Lick Trail was routed through Columbia, bringing in thousands of new settlers. Like Daniel Boone and his sons, who originally laid out the trail, many came from Virginia and Kentucky.

These newcomers valued education and

started several small colleges that were affiliated with churches. This established a tradition of higher learning in the city, which helped when the town lobbied to get the new state university. The cornerstone for the University of Missouri, the first state university west of the Mississippi River, was laid on July 4, 1840, and the first two men were graduated in 1843. Today, up to 3,800 undergraduates, 1,190 graduate students, 290 doctoral students, and 260 special degree students are graduated from Mizzou yearly. The university also has campuses at St. Louis, Kansas City, and Rolla. Stephens College, also in Columbia, is the oldest women's college west of the Mississippi.

One early leader of Columbia who fancied horse races had a law passed that prohibited racing on the main street except on Saturday. On that day, women and children were warned to stay out of the way because the men needed the straightest avenue in town for their weekend races.

Putting Her Stamp on the Job

Mrs. Richard Gentry, wife of a Columbia mayor who was killed in the Seminole Indian Wars in Florida, was named postmistress of Columbia in 1837. She held the position for thirty years, one of the first women to hold such an important job in the United States. ■

Gateway to the West

At the eastern edge of Missouri, where the Missouri River joins the Mississippi, is St. Louis, marked by the soaring grace of the Gateway Arch. At 630 feet high (192 m) the arch memorializes the country's westward expansion. St. Louis was the major jumping-off point for pioneers, traders, and soldiers. Reminders of the city's early days can be seen in two rooms in the Old Courthouse, renovated to look as they did in the mid-nineteenth century.

St. Louis has always been an economic powerhouse because of its location. It is the corporate headquarters for Monsanto chemical company, Ralston Purina feeds, Anheuser-Busch brewery,

The Gateway Arch

McDonnell-Douglas Aircraft, and other firms. The St. Louis Walk of Fame along Delmar Boulevard honors more than fifty notable city residents. Bronze stars and plaques tell of the accomplishments of local celebrities such as rock musician Chuck Berry, baseball great Stan Musial, novelist Tennessee Williams, and jazz singer Josephine Baker.

St. Louis has a wonderfully varied array of museums. Interested in dogs? Try the Dog Museum. How about pinball games? Visit the National Video Game and Coin-Op Museum. There's also the fascinating Mercantile Money Museum, the Museum of Black Inventors, and the Holocaust Museum and Learning Center, as well as the spectacular new St. Louis Science Center. St. Louis has the oldest botanic garden in the United States too.

A star on the St. Louis Walk of Fame

The riverfront entertainment district where steamboats used to dock is named Laclede's Landing after an early settler. Old warehouses have been renovated and turned into trendy restaurants, upscale pubs, and popular nightclubs. Several riverboat casinos and even a floating McDonald's Restaurant are tied up along the riverfront below the Gateway Arch.

A light-rail system called MetroLink takes commuters throughout the city and back and forth across the Mississippi River from Illinois to St. Louis. This connection eases the traffic flow from the suburbs to the downtown business district. The century-old St. Louis Union Station has been turned into restaurants and shops.

St. Charles is a northern suburb of St. Louis. It was Missouri's first capital from 1821 to 1826, providing a temporary site for the state's lawmakers until Jefferson City was ready. St. Charles was the starting point for the Lewis and Clark Expedition. A museum in town tells of the explorers' travels.

St. Louis First Facts

In 1818, St. Louis University, started by the Roman Catholic Church, was the first university founded west of the Mississippi River.

The Old Courthouse in St. Louis has the first cast-iron dome ever built. The picturesque building was under construction from 1839 to 1862.

In 1856, the city hosted the first major horse show in the United States.

The Eads Bridge (above) crossing the Mississippi River was the first arched steel-truss bridge in the world; completed in 1874.

The first successful parachute jump from an airplane took place in 1912 on the grounds of Jefferson Barracks.

St. Louis surgeon Dr. Evan Graham performed the first lung cancer operation in 1933. ■

About halfway down the length of the state from St. Louis but still on the Mississippi River is Cape Girardeau, one of Missouri's oldest cities. It began as a trading post about 1705 and was the site of several Union forts built during the Civil War to keep the river free from Confederate gunboats. Some people think that the South begins at Cape Girardeau.

One of the old shops in St. Charles

Ozark Cities

Springfield, Missouri's third-largest city, was founded in 1830. Its size and location have earned it the title of the Queen of the Ozarks. The southwestern Missouri community has always been a major regional transportation and commercial hub. Many rail lines converge here, and at one time the St. Louis and San Francisco Railway was the city's largest employer. Today, most people work for chemical, electrical machinery, and printing companies. Springfield is the leading religious center of the Ozarks area, with more than 150 churches and several Bible colleges. The Assembly of God world headquarters is also located here.

Branson, one of Missouri's small towns, has become a big name worldwide. This town, located south of Springfield, is Missouri's answer to Nashville, Tennessee, as a music city. This Ozark town has numerous country-western theaters. Busloads of tourists arrive daily to line up for shows at the Blackwood Family Theater, the Baldnobbers Jamboree Show, and the 76 Music Hall, among others. Silver Dollar City is one of the United States's largest amusement parks, developed from an old mining town.

As you can see, Missouri's cities are alive and vibrant.

Chapter Seven

"Show-Me" Government

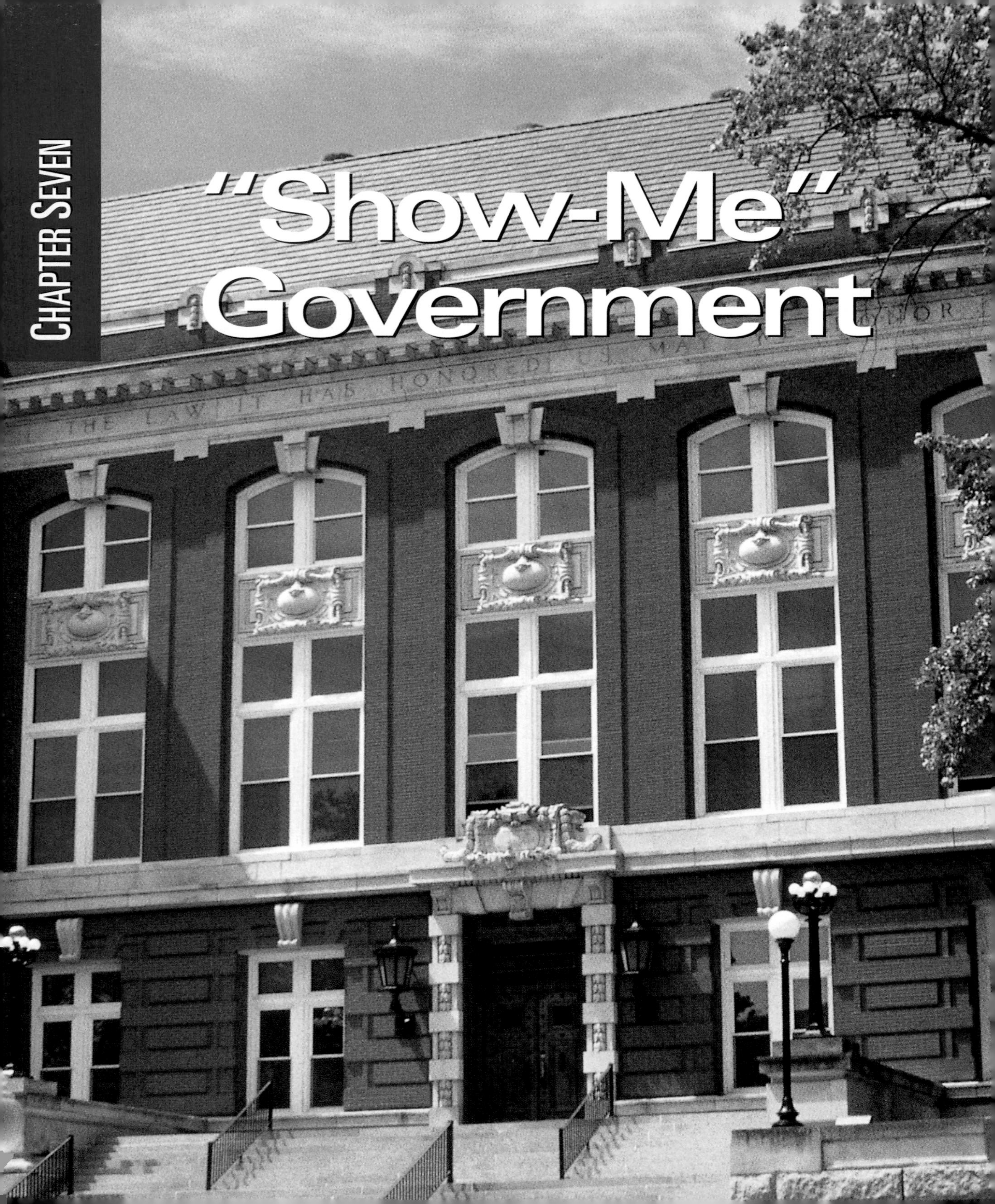

Politics in Missouri has always been a down-to-earth affair, with local issues ballooning into the national arena. For instance, the Missouri Compromise was an act passed by the U. S. Congress in 1820 that allowed Missouri to become a slave state but outlawed slavery in the Louisiana Purchase north of latitude 36° 31'. This was one of the first great debates over slavery in the United States, with legislators trying to maintain a political balance between free and slave states.

Tom Pendergast

The Bad with the Good

On all levels, Missourians love a good electoral fight. The state's political leaders have always been a tough-minded bunch, putting their own stamp on history. Some politicians were so powerful it seemed as though the candidates they wanted were automatically elected, as if by a machine. The term "political machine" came to mean this kind of behind-the-scenes politics. One of the most newsworthy machine politicians was Tom Pendergast, the undisputed boss of Kansas City from 1924 until 1939. His machine ended when he was imprisoned for tax evasion.

The plain-talking Democrat Harry S. Truman of Independence got his start working with Pendergast and used that rough-and-tumble political experience to good advantage. He became a judge, a U.S. senator, vice president, and finally president. He rose above his

Opposite: The Missouri supreme court

President for a Day

Missouri senator David Rice Atchison became president of the United States for one day in 1849. Atchison was acting as president of the Senate when the terms of President James K. Polk and Vice President George Dallas officially ended at noon on Sunday, March 4. However, President-elect Zachary Taylor (left), who was very religious, would not take the oath of office on a Sunday. So Atchison, as the highest-ranking senator, served from noon on that Sunday, until 11:30 A.M. the following day—Monday, March 5—when Taylor was finally sworn in.

A monument to Atchison in his hometown of Plattsburg honors the nation's "president for a day." In 1933, the U.S. Constitution was changed to put the inauguration of a new president on January 20. ■

political beginnings to lead the country at the end of World War II and help the United States through the Korean War. Truman is considered to have been one of the United States's best chief executives. The state celebrates his birthday every year on May 9 with a legal holiday.

Missouri's Constitution

Missouri's state governmental structure is similar to that of other states. The rules and principles of managing Missouri's affairs are described in its constitution. So, too, are the rights of the individual, similar to those guaranteed by the Bill of Rights in the U.S. Constitution.

The current Missouri document was adopted in 1945. However, three previous constitutions were written in 1820, 1865, and 1875. Every twenty years, the state's citizens vote on whether to call a convention to amend this important document.

The constitution can be amended in two ways. A majority of the members of the state legislature can advocate an amendment, or

8 percent of the voters in two-thirds of the state's congressional districts can sign a petition proposing a change. To become part of the constitution, an amendment must then be okayed by a majority of the people voting on the measure.

Almost

In 1911, progressive Congressman James Beauchamp ("Champ") Clark (right, with Mrs. Clark and son Bennett) of Pike County was named speaker of the U.S. House of Representatives. He was the only Missourian ever to hold this top spot.

The 1912 Democratic national convention almost chose Clark as its presidential candidate. It took forty-six ballots by the convention's delegates before the nomination went to Woodrow Wilson, then the liberal governor of New Jersey. Clark, a loyal party man, then actively campaigned for Wilson, who won the election.

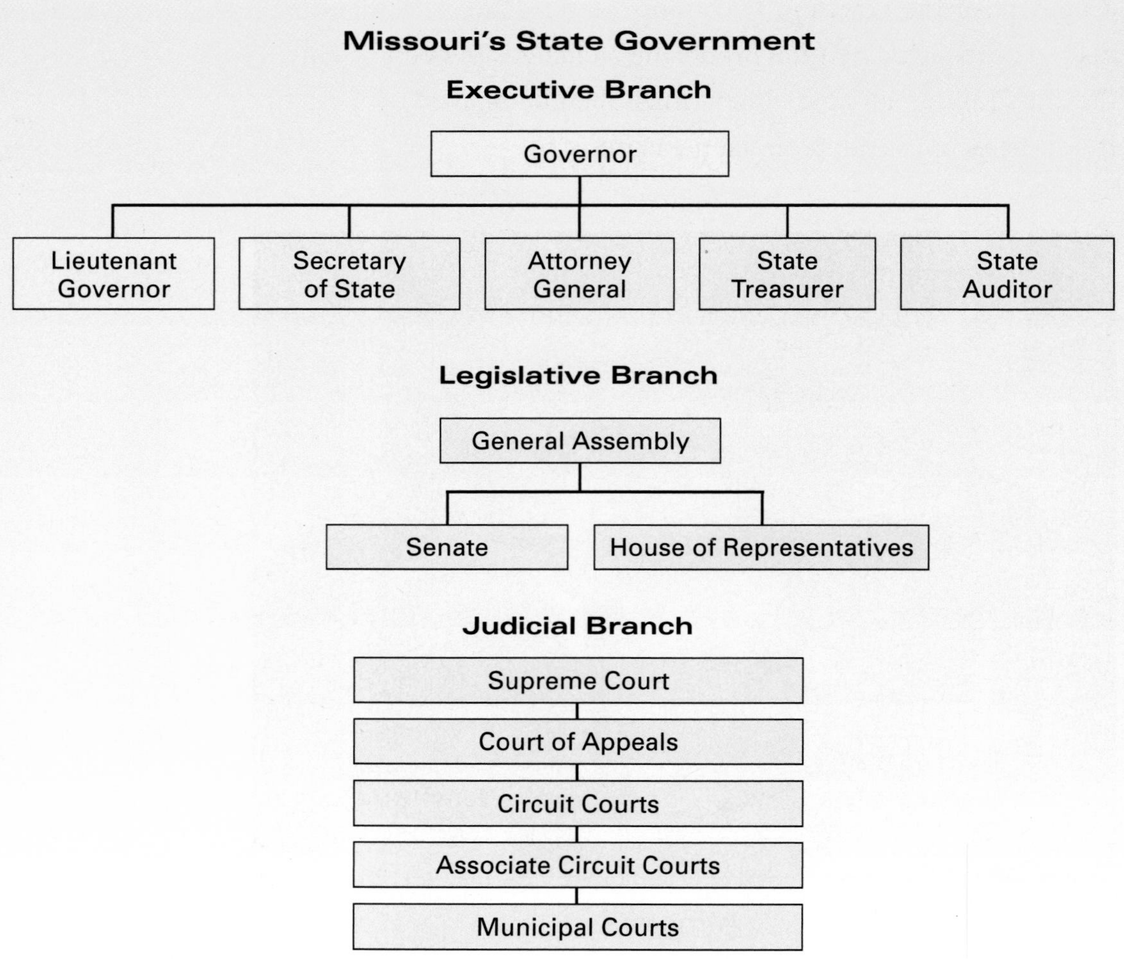

Working on behalf of Missouri at the federal level are two U.S. senators and nine members of the House of Representatives. Their job is to represent the state's citizens in Washington, D.C.

Missouri's political leaders are highly respected. They range from Thomas Hart Benton, one of the state's first senators, to reformers and social activists Frank Blair and Carl Schurz. Representative Richard Gephardt, a St. Louis Democrat and the leading Democrat in Congress today, has often been mentioned as a presidential candidate.

Three Divisions of Government

There are three divisions of government on the state level—an executive branch, a two-house legislature, and a judicial branch. The legislature makes the laws; the executive branch, headed by the governor, carries them out; and the judicial branch is the court system. All three branches are headquartered in Jefferson City, the capital.

The executive branch is made up of the governor, lieutenant governor, secretary of state, attorney general, state treasurer, and state auditor. All these positions are filled by elections. With the senate's approval, the governor chooses department directors to coordinate day-to-day operations of the state. The sixteen offices to which directors are appointed include education, natural resources, agriculture, and transportation.

The legislative branch, called the general assembly, makes the laws that govern the state. It is divided into the senate and the house of representatives. There are thirty-four Missouri senators. Each senator is elected for four years and can serve no more than two terms. To qualify as a Missouri senator, a person must be thirty years old, a registered Missouri voter for three years, and a resident of the area he or she will represent.

There are 163 members of the Missouri House of Representatives. They serve two-year terms and can be re-elected only four times. To be elected to the house, a candidate must be twenty-four years old, a registered voter for two years, and a resident in his or her district.

The Missouri General Assembly in session

The legislature meets once every year, from January into May. During this time, legislators discuss and make new laws or update existing Missouri laws. Special sessions can also be called by the governor or by three-fourths of either the senate or house.

Missouri's governor has to be at least thirty years old, a U.S. citizen for fifteen years, and a Missouri resident for ten years. The governor appoints and removes government officials, vetoes bills passed by the legislature, pardons convicted criminals, and commands the state's military forces.

The courts interpret the laws passed by the legislature. The supreme court, with seven judges, is the most important court in the state because it makes the final decision if a case decided in a lower court is disputed. Every two years, the justices select one of their members to be chief justice. The state court of appeals is made up of the Western District in Kansas City, the Southern District in

Governors of Missouri

Name	Party	Term	Name	Party	Term
Alexander McNair	Dem.-Rep.	1820–1824	Albert P. Morehouse	Dem.	1887–1889
Frederick Bates	Dem.-Rep	1824–1825	David R. Francis	Dem.	1889–1893
Abraham J. Williams	Dem.-Rep.	1825–1826	William Joel Stone	Dem.	1893–1897
John Miller	Dem.-Rep.	1826–1832	Lon V. Stephens	Dem.	1897–1901
Daniel Dunklin	Dem.	1832–1836	Alexander M. Dockery	Dem.	1901–1905
Lilburn W. Boggs	Dem.	1836–1840	Joseph W. Folk	Dem.	1905–1909
Thomas Reynolds	Dem.	1840–1844	Herbert S. Hadley	Rep.	1909–1913
Meredith M. Marmaduke	Dem.	1844	Elliott W. Major	Dem.	1913–1917
			Frederick D. Gardner	Dem.	1917–1921
John C. Edwards	Dem.	1844–1848	Arthur M. Hyde	Rep.	1921–1925
Austin A. King	Dem.	1848–1853	Sam A. Baker	Rep.	1925–1929
Sterling Price	Dem.	1853–1857	Henry S. Caulfield	Rep.	1929–1933
Trusten Polk	Dem.	1857	Guy B. Park	Dem.	1933–1937
Hancock Lee Jackson	Dem.	1857	Lloyd C. Stark	Dem.	1937–1941
Robert M. Stewart	Dem.	1857–1861	Forrest C. Donnell	Rep.	1941–1945
Claiborne F. Jackson	Dem.	1861	Phil M. Donnelly	Dem.	1945–1949
Hamilton R. Gamble	Union	1861–1864	Forrest Smith	Dem.	1949–1953
Willard P. Hall	Union	1864–1865	Phil M. Donnelly	Dem.	1953–1957
Thomas C. Fletcher	Rad. Rep.	1865–1869	James T. Blair Jr.	Dem.	1957–1961
Joseph W. McClurg	Rad. Rep.	1869–1871	John M. Dalton	Dem.	1961–1965
B. Gratz Brown	Lib. Rep.	1871–1873	Warren E. Hearnes	Dem.	1965–1973
Silas Woodson	Dem.	1873–1875	Christopher S. Bond	Rep.	1973–1977
Charles H. Hardin	Dem.	1875–1877	Joseph P. Teasdale	Dem.	1977–1981
John S. Phelps	Dem.	1877–1881	Christopher S. Bond	Rep.	1981–1985
Thomas T. Crittenden	Dem.	1881–1885	John Ashcroft	Rep.	1985–1993
John S. Marmaduke	Dem.	1885–1887	Mel Carnahan	Dem.	1993–

Springfield, and the Eastern District in St. Louis. The governor appoints the judges of the supreme court and the appeals courts for twelve-year terms. Voters approve appointed judges in the next general election. There are also circuit courts, associate circuit courts, and municipal courts.

Fishing Tradition

For years, the Missouri secretary of state has officially opened trout season in the state by firing a starter pistol at 6:30 A.M. on March 1. Secretary Rebecca ("Bekki") McDowell Cook performed the 1999 honors. ■

Missouri's State Song
"Missouri Waltz"

The "Missouri Waltz" became the state song on June 30, 1949. The origin of the song is unclear, although historians generally agree it was first printed around 1912 by Frederick Knight Logan, who obtained the melody from orchestra leader John Valentine Eppel. In 1914, the Forster Publishing Company bought the rights to the melody. Lyrics were added by Jim Shannon.

The song became popular when Harry S. Truman became president. He often played the tune on the White House piano.

Hush-a-bye, ma baby, slumber-time is comin' soon;
Rest yo' head upon my breast while Mommy hums a tune;
The sandman is callin' where shadows are fallin',
While the soft breezes sigh as in days long gone by.

Way down in Missouri where I heard this melody,
When I was a little child upon my Mommy's knee;
The old folks were hummin'; their banjoes were strummin';
So sweet and low.

Strum, strum, strum, strum, strum,
Seems I hear those banjoes playin' once again,
Hum, hum, hum, hum, hum,
That same old plaintive strain.

Hear that mournful melody,
It just haunts you the whole day long,
And you wander in dreams back to Dixie, it seems,
When you hear that old time song.

Hush-a-bye, ma baby, go to sleep on Mommy's knee,
Journey back to Dixieland in dreams again with me;
It seems like your Mommy is there once again,
And the old folks were strummin' that same old refrain.

Way down in Missouri where I learned this lullaby,
When the stars were blinkin' and the moon was climbin' high,
Seems I hear voices low, as in days long ago,
Singin' hush-a-bye.

Missouri's counties

Local Government

On the local level of government, there are 114 counties in Missouri. In addition, the city of St. Louis, which is separate from St. Louis County, has the power of a county. In each county, three county commissioners usually act as chief administrators. Other county offices include a sheriff, recorder of deeds, coroner, surveyor, public administrator, treasurer, assessor, prosecuting attorney, and tax collector. Most Missouri cities have a mayor-council form of government.

Missouri State Symbols

State tree: Flowering dogwood Chosen on June 20, 1955, the dogwood tree grows well in Missouri's rocky Ozarks, reaching no more than 40 feet (12 m) tall or 18 inches (46 cm) around its trunk. The dogwood blossoms are small greenish-yellow clusters of flowers framed by four white petals. In autumn, the tips of the leaves turn red or orange and bright red fruit grows on the tree.

State flower: Hawthorn Declared the state flower on March 16, 1923, the hawthorn is commonly called the red haw or wild haw. It is a member of the rose family. The blossoms form white clusters in April and May. More than 75 types of hawthorn grow in Missouri.

State fossil: Crinoid This relative of the starfish was selected in 1989. Starfishlike crinoids lived in the waters that covered Missouri 20 million years ago.

State bird: Eastern bluebird Adopted on March 30, 1927, the eastern bluebird is is a songbird noted for its blue head and back and its rust-colored breast. In winter it migrates farther south.

State folk dance: Square dance European immigrants brought courtship and folk dances to the United States, which eventually developed into the modern-day square dance. Missouri adopted it as the state folk dance on May 31, 1995.

State musical instrument: Fiddle When settlers and traders introduced the fiddle, or violin, to Missouri in the 1700s, people found it easy to transport, simple to learn, and suited to many different types of music. It became the state's official instrument on July 17, 1987.

State tree nut: Black walnut This nut is used for a wide variety of products such as ice cream, metal cleaning, and dynamite filler. It's no surprise, then, that an industrial state like Missouri would adopt it as the state tree nut. It became official on July 9, 1990.

State insect: Honeybee This insect can be found throughout Missouri, and its honey is harvested by beekeepers statewide. It became the state insect on July 3, 1985.

State animal: Missouri mule A cross between a horse and donkey, the mule is a strong animal and has been used throughout Missouri's history by pioneers, farmers, and troops during the two World Wars. It became the state animal on May 31, 1995.

State rock: Mozarkite Mostly located in Benton County, mozarkite is purple, red, or green, and is often used for jewelry. It became the state rock on July 21, 1967.

State mineral: Galena To give additional notice to Missouri's position as the main lead-producing state in the United States, legislators named galena as the official mineral on July 21, 1967. Galena, the major source of lead ore, is found in southwestern Missouri. ■

The State Flag and Seal

The flag has three horizontal stripes of red, white, and blue surrounding the state seal. The seal is set in a circle of twenty-four stars to show that Missouri is the twenty-fourth state. The flag was designed by Cape Girardeau resident Marie Oliver and was adopted in 1913. The seal features two grizzly bears holding a circlet reading "United we stand, divided we fall." The bears stand on a scroll inscribed with the state motto. The shield is divided in two and stands in the center of the seal to symbolize that Missouri is linked to, but independent of, the federal government. Twenty-four stars are on top of the seal. The design of the seal was signed into law on January 11, 1822. ■

Chapter Eight

In the Center of It All

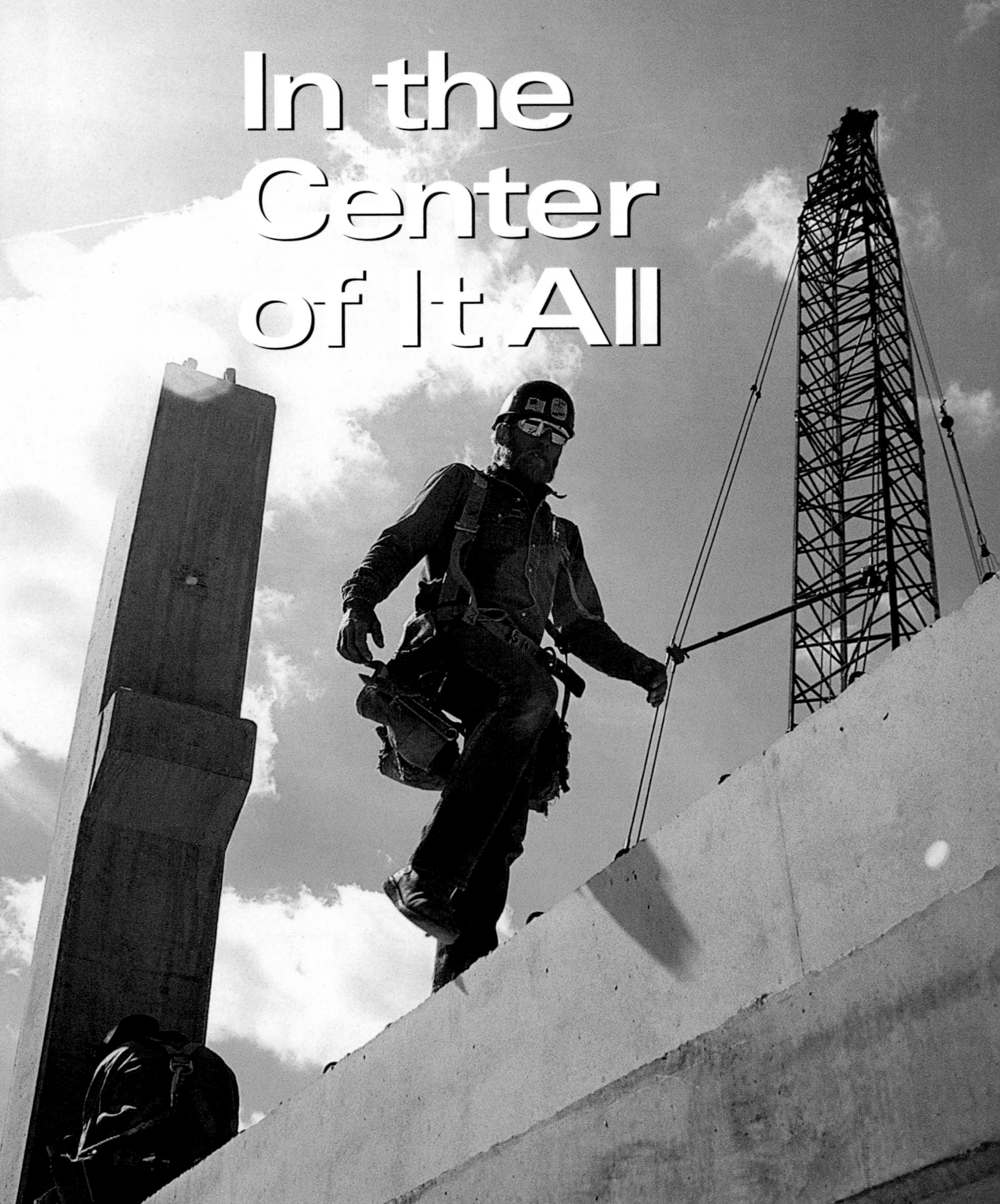

Kirkwood's Amtrak station

Being in the center of everything has its advantages. About 43 percent of the country's population is within a day's drive or about a 500-mile (800-km) radius of Missouri. That covers at least twenty states. More than $700 billion is spent for retail merchandise throughout this area. That accounts for 41 percent of all sales in the United States! No wonder Missourians are glad to live where they do. They have almost unlimited markets for their products.

Because Missouri sits in the heart of the country, it is a transportation, warehousing, and manufacturing hub of the nation. The state's modern network of highways, harbors, and airports provides a strong support base for moving goods.

Traveling On

Ten interstate highways and 121,000 miles (194,700 km) of state and federal roads allow great market access. St. Louis and Kansas City are two of the country's largest truck terminals. Instead of wagon trains, monster eighteen-wheelers haul furniture, cars, propane gas, lumber, fruit, and computer equipment in and out of the state's warehouses. More than 65,000 truck trailers are registered in Missouri.

Opposite: Construction workers in Kansas City

Celebrating Missouri

In 1915, the Missouri General Assembly established a Missouri Day. The purpose of the holiday was to encourage state residents to reflect on the state's diverse economy, the implications of its history, and the many achievements of its citizens. In 1969, the third Wednesday of October was chosen for the official celebration.

With 7,000 miles (11,200 km) of track, the state is also a railroad center. Missouri ranks tenth in the nation for total rail mileage and rail traffic, with its nine major railroads providing inexpensive, efficient shipping.

Travelers using the international airports in Kansas City and St. Louis can fly to London, Paris, Bangkok, and other cities around the world. Lambert-St. Louis Airport is the fifteenth-busiest airport in the United States and the twenty-fourth-busiest in the world, with more than 27 million passengers using its facilities each year. There are eight other commercial airports in the state.

Even before the steamboat days, Missouri's rivers were important for hauling freight. Fourteen ports and more than 1,000 miles (1,600 km) of navigable waterways make it easy to utilize the state's harbors along the Missouri, Mississippi, and other accessible rivers.

Changing planes at the Lambert-St. Louis Airport

The Industrial Mix

Missouri's industrial scene is like a great melting pot. Missourians mix chemicals, tune aircraft engines, build automobiles, and brew beer. They are graphic artists, lawyers, computer scientists, insurance agents, realtors, window washers, farmers, pilots, doctors, professors, service-station attendants, street sweepers, mechanics, and bakers.

Many of the state's companies are among the largest in their fields. Hallmark, Inc., of Kansas City produces greeting cards. St. Louis's Monsanto Company is a giant in

Tap In!

Anheuser-Busch, Inc., is the world's largest brewery. The company is headquartered in St. Louis, with sales of its products worldwide. Starting as a tiny brewery bought by Eberhard Anheuser, it was developed by his son-in-law Adolphus Busch. The corporate name shows up in many places. Dedicated parade watchers love seeing the Budweiser Clydesdales prance past, huge and proud horses with jangling harnesses. Television viewers are familiar with the company's talking frogs and lizards in its commercials.

Anheuser-Busch also owns nine major theme parks around the country. Four of them are Sea Worlds, and the rest are Busch Gardens. Careful of its image, Anheuser-Busch sponsors many programs to reduce underage drinking and to encourage responsible use of alcohol. ■

chemical research. Procter & Gamble Paper in Jackson is one of the state's major employers. Procter & Gamble also owns Folger Coffee of Kansas City. The headquarters of Ralston Purina, the animal-food specialists, are on "Checkerboard Square" in St. Louis.

These companies are all American, but in 1998, Missouri also had 274 foreign-owned business sites. Foreign firms employed a total of 54,644 Missouri residents.

Eager to Work

More than 68 percent of Missouri's nonfarm jobs are in the wholesale and retail trade, services, and manufacturing. This accounted for 1,708,900 jobs in the mid-1990s. Other nonagricultural jobs employed 811,500 persons. Construction, mining, banking, transportation, and government are the leading employers. As the nature of jobs has slowly changed from a majority of blue-collar laborers to more white-collar service workers, union membership declined from 20.8 percent in 1983 to 15.4 percent in 1996.

Like the rest of the United States, Missouri suffered through the Great Depression of the 1930s. This was an international financial slump in which banks failed, farms were lost, and businesses closed. The economy rebounded during World War II as the state's manufacturing plants went into overtime for the war effort.

Making Stetson hats in St. Louis

Another business push occurred in the late 1980s and early 1900s, with 2,296 new factories being constructed and older facilities improved or expanded. This opened up 118,201 additional jobs. In that one decade, more than $738 million was invested annually in the state's manufacturing sector.

Even now, an average of 90 new industrial companies starts up each year, bringing in about 5,000 new positions. Every year, some 140 firms expand their operations, adding almost 8,000 additional jobs. Since 1984, almost $7.4 billion has been invested in

What Missouri Grows, Manufactures, and Mines

Agriculture	Mining	Manufacturing
Beef cattle	Coal	Chemicals
Corn	Lead	Electrical equipment
Hay	Limestone	Food products
Hogs		Machinery
Soybeans		Metal products
		Printed materials
		Transportation equipment

improving the state's industries. In 1997, the average hourly wage in Missouri was $13.38, ranking it twenty-sixth nationwide.

Missourians are ready and eager to put in a good day's work. They are considered among the country's most stable, educated, and productive workforce. Much of this is a result of their training. Fifty-eight vocational-technical schools, fifteen junior colleges, and ten four-year colleges and universities offer programs to make sure students are ready for the world of work. In addition, people take advantage of occupational benefits. Many employees seek out on-the-job training opportunities and after-work classes to improve their skills.

The McDonnell-Douglas Aircraft factory in St. Louis

Help for Business

The state government works closely with Missouri businesses. It has a computerized job service to link employers with prospective workers. It also offers free business development assistance in many areas. For instance, if a Missouri company wants to send its goods overseas, an international business specialist for the state can help deal with all the rules and regulations.

Missouri also operates three Centers for Advanced Technology at the state's top universities, as well as the Missouri Technology Corporation. These research organizations coordinate development efforts through science, technology, and education. There are also four state-operated "innovative centers" that provide low-cost workspace for people starting their own businesses. These entrepreneurs share secretarial and other business costs, keeping expenses low for a start-up company.

Tourists navigating their way through Missouri's sites

Professional organizations such as the St. Louis Minority Business Council assist minority-owned companies. The council is tied into a national network that helps create more markets for its member firms. The state Department of Economic Development even has a special hot line for minority-owned business, with experts able to answer questions quickly on a range of issues from taxes to transportation.

Using the Rich Land

Agriculture is a very strong component of the state's economy. Missouri's rich soils and temperate climate make it a near-perfect place for farmers. The state is proud of its reputation as a leading livestock producer. Livestock accounts for 56 percent of the state's agricultural income. The mooing of dairy and beef cattle and the oinking of pigs is music to the state's financial ears. The clucking of chickens is part of that symphony, with poultry-processing contributing to Missouri's $4 billion annual agricultural business. Aquaculture, the cultivating of fish and other aquatic products, is a growing part of that healthy climate, as demands increase for fish as food, ornamental uses, and bait.

Missouri's varied topography is a bonus for its agricultural community. The Ozark hills yield timber and provide pastureland. More than a million acres of flatland are planted in corn. Cotton and rice grow well along the fertile bottomlands—the areas that flood—of the Mississippi and Missouri Rivers. Sorghum (a grain crop that looks like corn) and wheat grow well throughout the state. Delicious apples, melons, and other fruits and vegetables are found everywhere. Soybeans are Missouri's largest cash crop, with thousands of acres in the southeast and across the northern tier of the state planted in the protein-rich plant.

Corn harvesting

Fair Fun

Here are some more figures. Missouri produces 7 percent of the United States' soybeans and turkeys and 8 percent of its sorghum. It has 5 percent of the country's hog farms and 6 percent of its cattle ranches. Everyone is proud of this bounty. Missourians celebrate their good farming fortune at more than 160 county fairs.

The Missouri State Fair, held each August in Sedalia, is loads of fun. The fair is a grand collection of contented cows, crazy carnival rides, cotton candy, and cream puffs.

Missouri Farm Facts

Second in the United States in hay production
Sixth-leading state in beef cattle
Sixth in rice production
Ninth in corn production
Twelfth in milk production
Sixteenth in red meat production ■

The Missouri Mule

The Missouri State Fair is the best place to see the Missouri mule, the state animal. The mule, which is the offspring of a donkey and a horse, is noted for its strength, toughness, intelligence—and its stubbornness. Missourians brag that the mule has attributes just like them! For generations, Missourians used mules to help log forests, mine coal, and haul goods to market. They even helped in wartime. Of the more than 232,000 mules used by the United States during World War I, most came from Missouri. Today, tractors have replaced mules on farms, and the rugged, long-eared animals are bred for show. ■

Among the people who come to the Missouri State Fair are buyers from all over the world. Missouri's farms produced $4 billion worth of products in the mid-1990s. Of that, more than $1.2 billion was sold internationally. A restaurant in Germany may serve beef raised in Missouri. A Norwegian baker might use Missouri grain. A Canadian grocer could stock Missouri watermelons.

One of Missouri's many cattle farms

Showing Off the Show-Me State

Not all of Missouri's business is tied to making products and growing produce. Tourism is consistently one of Missouri's top three moneymakers. More visitors are discovering the state's charm. The "Wake Up to Missouri" marketing campaign lets travelers know what the state offers in attractions, activities, and accommodations. In the mid-1990s, tourism spending had reached almost $10 billion and was steadily climbing. This spending generated more than $888 million in state taxes, as well as $471 million in revenue for local governments.

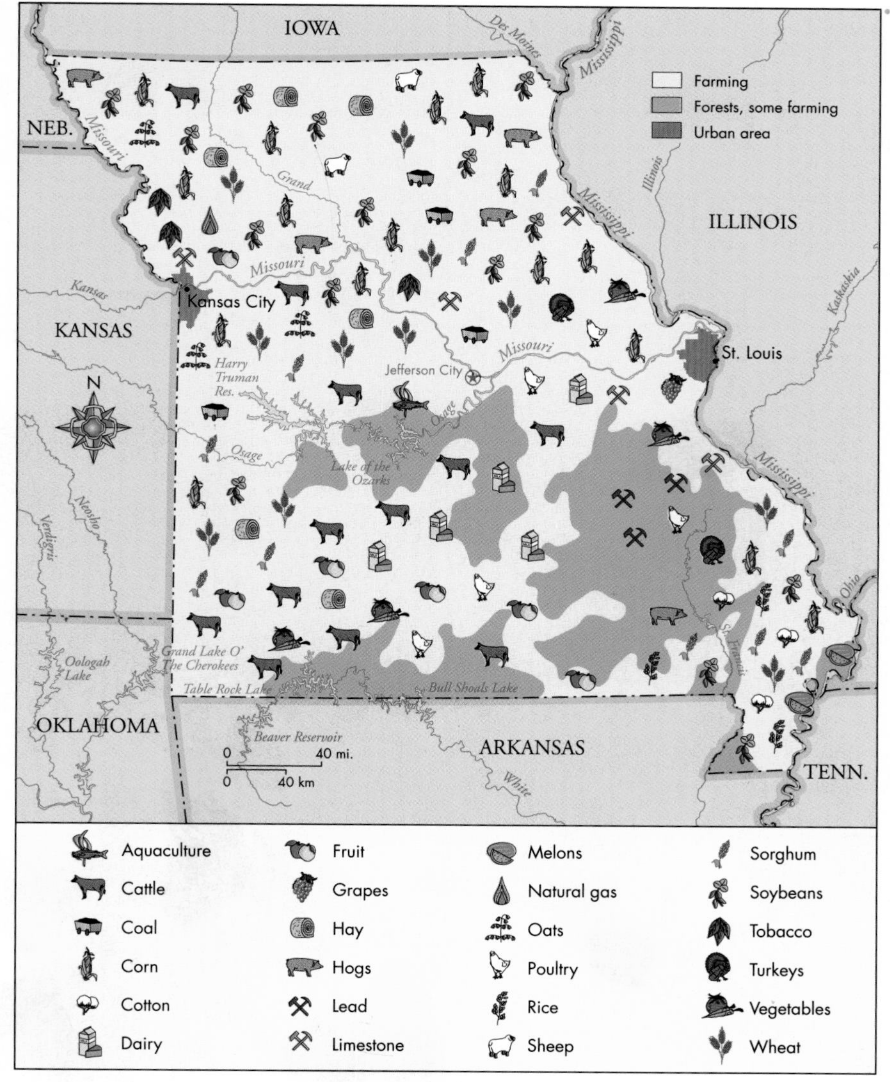

Missouri's natural resources

More than 261,000 persons were employed in tourism by the mid-1990s, accounting for 10 percent of all the state's jobs. Most of these were in small "mom-and-pop" operations, from motels to dude-ranches. Missourians are proud to show off their state.

Chapter Nine

The People of Change

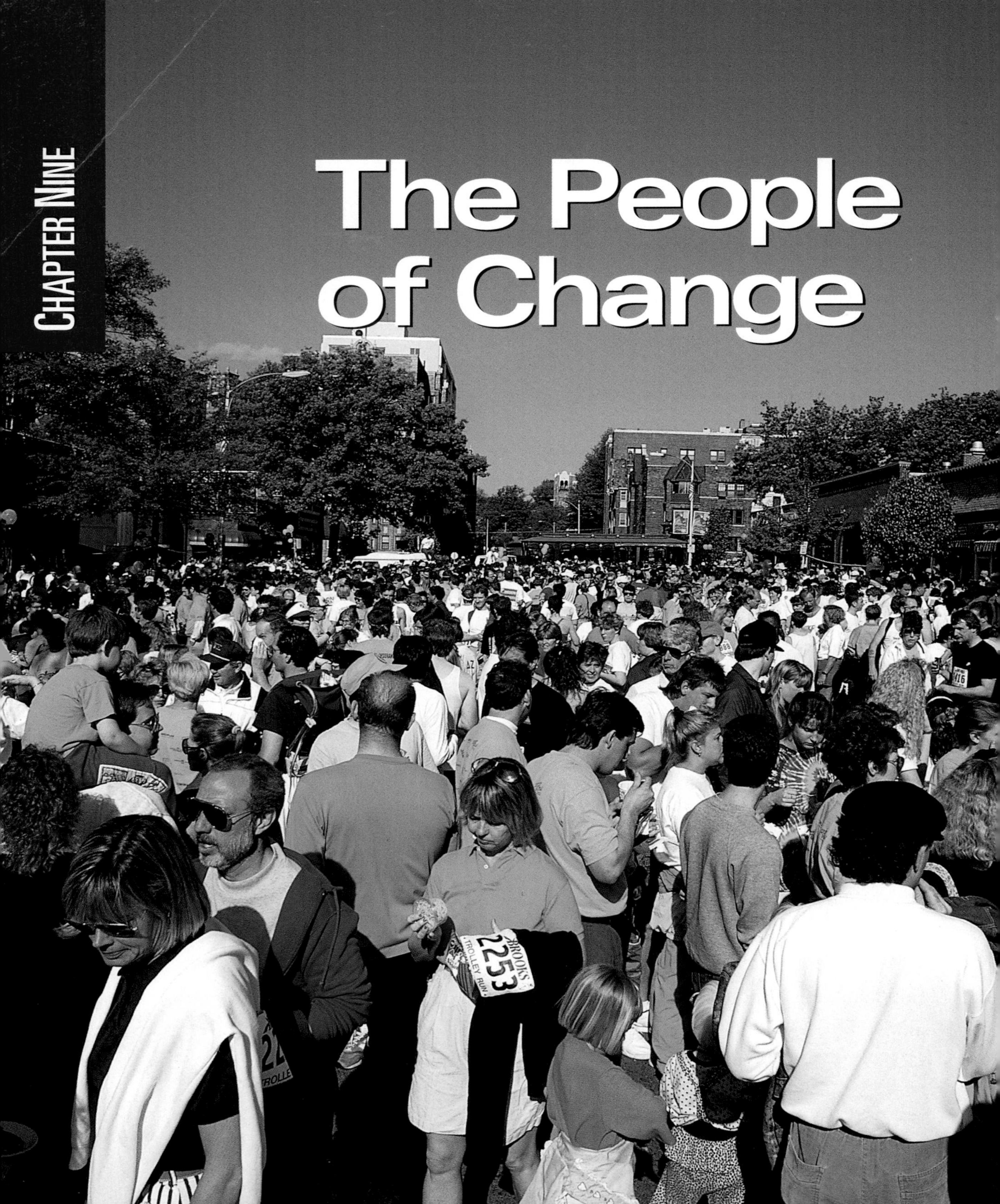

Paddling down the Meramec River

The Gateway Arch, towering over the St. Louis skyline, can be seen for miles. Whether the rising sun is mirrored on its eastern side or the setting sun on its western side, the arch is a magnet for the eye. The graceful structure, designed by world-famous architect Eero Saarinen, is officially called the Jefferson National Expansion Memorial. It represents the diversity of Missouri, as well as a passage to the West. The arch reminds us that the state has always been a crossroads for travelers, and the migrants to Missouri are as varied as the Old Country lands they leave behind.

From 1950 through 1960, only 31 of Missouri's 114 countries gained any population. During the next ten years, however, the population grew in 52 counties. The 1980 census, or population count, showed a head count of 4,916,758 in the state. The 1990 census counted 5,137,804 Missourians, showing that 62 counties had increased in population.

The total population of the Show-Me State was estimated to be 5,358,692 in 1996—an increase of 0.7 percent over the previous year. Such a jump in growth had not occurred in Missouri since the late 1960s and early 1970s.

Within Missouri, the population density is shifting. New residents flood the counties rimming St. Louis and Kansas City. Twenty-nine percent of all Missourians live in Boone, Buchanan,

Opposite: Crowds at the Kansas City Plaza Trolley Run

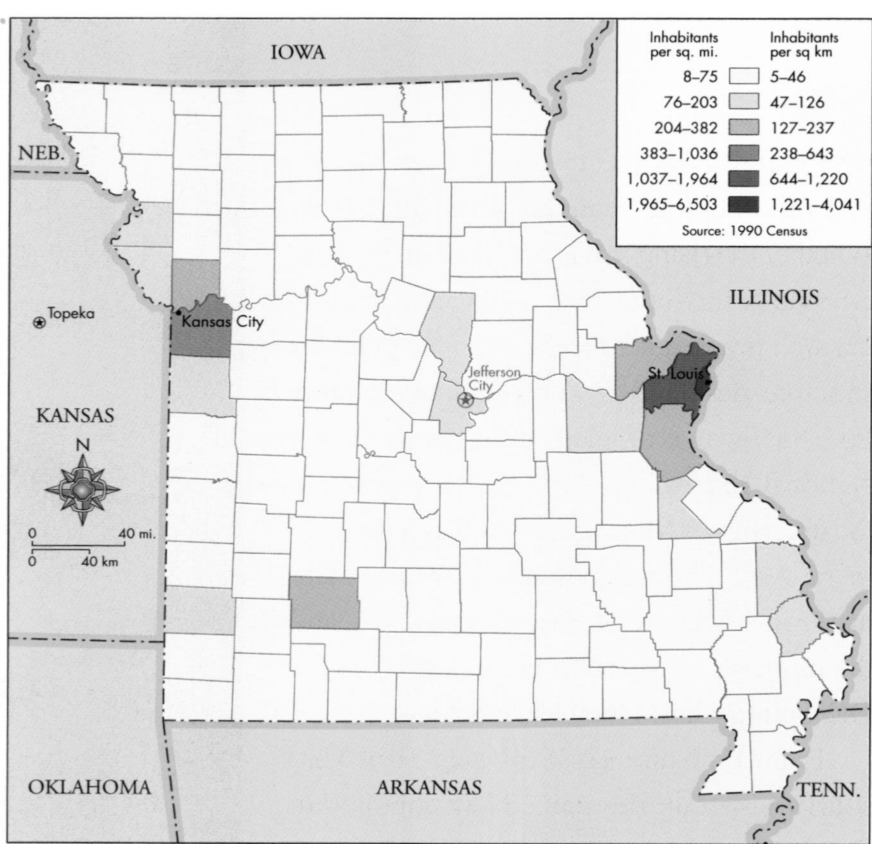

Missouri's population density

Greene, Jackson, and Jasper counties and in the city of St. Louis. However, some Missourians are moving back to rural areas. They love the natural springs, the shade trees, and the refreshing lakes. Retirees often move to the Ozarks to relax. Families look for an atmosphere where children can experience small-town life.

The Culturally Diverse State

From the mound-building ancients to immigrants searching for a place to call home, Missouri has long contained a variety of cultures. However, history has some unhappy stories. It took only a few generations from the time Europeans began to arrive until the

Native Americans were permanently pushed out of their lands. Unfortunately, treaties that were supposed to protect the Indian nations were constantly broken as the crush of settlers advanced steadily westward in search of land and opportunity.

Another big issue facing early Missourians was what to do about the thousands of African-Americans in their midst. From the area's earliest days, free blacks were reluctantly allowed to live in Missouri. But the bottom line was simple—black residents were considered second-class persons.

Not everyone agreed with this view, however. Missourians argued fiercely on street corners, in restaurants, in their homes, and in businesses about the black population. The North's victory in the Civil War and the subsequent freeing of slaves did not end the debate. For years, hate groups like the Ku Klux Klan actively worked to terrorize black citizens. There were murders, hangings, and race riots. Some Missourians fought to keep black people segregated, or separated from whites.

George Washington Carver

Maya Angelou

The Failure of Separation

In 1875, separate schools were established for the races, an unfortunate situation that lasted long into the civil rights era of the 1960s and 1970s. The schools for black students were rarely, if ever, as good as those for whites. Lack of a decent education kept many young blacks from achieving their full potential. Thirst for knowledge drove away many like the brilliant George Washington Carver.

Missouri's determined and proud black population overcame many obstacles. Some went on to become wonderful entertainers like Josephine Baker, or poets and activists like Maya Angelou.

The Amazing Scientist

Born to slave parents, probably in 1861, near Diamond Grove, George Washington Carver was forced to leave Missouri and go to Kansas and Iowa in search of a way to go to school. He was in his late twenties before he earned his high school diploma and he was thirty-two when he earned his master's degree in agricultural science.

This former slave spent most of his adult life teaching and researching at Tuskegee Institute in Alabama. His work helped to rebuild the South because he demonstrated that farmers who had depleted the soil by growing cotton could improve their land by growing peanuts, sweet potatoes, and soybeans. He also found many ways that those crops could be used, creating new markets for them. This innovative work by a former slave helped to improve the economies of the South. ■

Many went into medicine and law. Attorney Margaret Bush Wilson was among those who worked hard on behalf of her people. She served as chairman of the board for the National Association for the Advancement of Colored People in the late 1970s and early 1980s.

Others became political leaders. The first black senator in Missouri was Theodore D. McNeal, elected in 1960. He went on to become the president of the St. Louis Board of Police Commisioners. It wasn't long before African-Americans were making increasing political strides. By 1969, Missouri ranked second in the number of blacks serving in state and local government. In 1977, Gwen B. Gilles became the first black woman to serve in the Missouri senate. Numerous mayors, legislators, aldermen and alderwomen, and county executives were also elected. In 1994, about 12 percent of Missourians were African-Americans, Hispanics, and Asians. By the end of the 1990s, many African-Americans had found their rightful place in Missouri's society.

Newcomers Move In

From its first years, Missouri's white population was very mixed. Newcomers came into the region from the rural South, from the city slums of the Northeast, and from the hill country of Kentucky and Tennessee. This led to a colorful, if sometimes disturbing, blend of conservatism and individualism—a volatile mixture that affected life in the state for years. Even religions were sometimes at odds. Strict Baptist and Methodist traditions clashed with those of the more relaxed French Roman Catholic heritage. In the 1830s, members of the Church of Jesus Christ of Latter-day Saints—the Mormons—were persecuted because of their beliefs.

Population of Missouri's Major Cities (1990)

Kansas City	435,146
St. Louis	396,685
Springfield	140,494
Independence	112,301
St. Joseph	71,852
Columbia	69,101

The state's long-time residents often viewed the rising numbers of immigrants from overseas with alarm. Many Missourians feared their new neighbors because of their unfamiliar language and traditions. Acceptance often came slowly. But the newcomers were determined and they eventually made a positive mark on the state.

More than half of today's Missourians trace their heritage to a single ancestry group, primarily German or English. Thirty-four percent claim several ancestry groups.

The Missouri melting pot now includes Scottish truck drivers, Polish restaurant owners, Italian bakers, Norwegian business leaders, Thai computer software programmers, and Honduran retailers. Germans have been in Missouri longest and in the greatest numbers.

An Italian bakery in St. Louis

Traditional German dancers at a Missouri festival

By 1850, one out of three St. Louis residents was German. Of foreign-born Missourians in the early days, half came from Germany. Their legacy is found in town names like New Melle, Wittenberg, and Westphalia. Their faith affected religious life, with one group founding the Lutheran Church–Missouri Synod, a more conservative and stricter branch of the Lutheran Church.

Tens of thousands of Irish people also came to live in Missouri, retaining links with their homeland. Former Irish Prime Minister John Bruton, whose distant cousins farm in the state, visits regularly to say hello. The regional headquarters of the Irish American Chamber of Commerce in the USA (ICCUSA) is based in St. Louis. The Irish Foreign Service even has a city law firm acting as an honorary consular office. The University of Missouri and Ireland's Department of Agriculture have launched a crop-study program that tracks harvests on a worldwide scale.

Because Missouri was once a Spanish colony, there has always been a Hispanic presence in the state. Today, Missouri citizens hail from Puerto Rico, Peru, Honduras, Spain, Mexico, Brazil, Colombia, Chile, and other Latin American countries. At the turn of the century, Ricardo Flores Magón, a prominent Mexican journalist, lived in St. Louis. His *Regeneración* newspaper helped to overthrow a brutal dictatorship in his homeland.

Landmarks and Baseball

Gyo Obata, a Japanese-American who was born, raised, and educated in St. Louis, co-founded an architectural firm in that city in 1955. His company has designed many of the city's landmark buildings, such as One Metropolitan Square, the St. Louis Convention Center, and the St. Louis Zoo. He also spearheaded restoration of the old Union Station, turning it into a fascinating mall. In Independence, he designed the new Temple of the Reorganized Church of Jesus Christ of Latter-day Saints.

Far away from St. Louis, his firm designed the Baltimore Orioles' baseball park at Camden Yards in Maryland. Since the Orioles were originally the St. Louis Browns, this choice of an architect seems fitting.

Asians, too, have a long Missouri link. Between 1850 and 1870, a sizable population of Chinese worked in St. Louis in laundries and toiled as laborers. In the 1990s, more than 15,000 Americans of Chinese descent lived in the city. Filipinos, Thai, Vietnamese, Cambodians, Indians, and other Asians also call Missouri their home today. They still celebrate their traditional holidays and feasts much as they did in their homelands.

In recent years, traditional family life has been changing in Missouri as it has elsewhere, although the 1990 census recorded that more than 84 percent of Missourians continue to live in some kind of family situation. Like most families across the country, Missouri's are a mixed bunch. The idea of who makes up a family unit is changing. An increasing number of independent Missourians over sixty-five live alone. Single-parent families have also increased while some families have a mom and a dad. Some families include grandparents or step-parents, and some children have step-, half-, or adopted siblings.

Educating Missouri and the World

The Missouri State Department of Education oversees public schooling, and a strict separation of church and state is maintained in the school system. Eighty-five percent of all students attend public schools, but many youngsters in the bigger cities attend parochial, or private, schools—mostly Catholic or Lutheran. Public elementary and secondary schools were established in 1839 and are administered by local boards.

Schools around the state were desegregated after a 1954 Supreme Court decision. Like many big cities, St. Louis, Kansas City, and others have had a tough time mixing black and white students to everyone's benefit.

The oldest state university west of the Mississippi River is the University of Missouri, founded in Columbia in 1839. Today, there are also campuses at Rolla, Kansas City, and St. Louis. Other state universities in Missouri are Northwest Missouri at Maryville, Southeast Missouri at Cape Girardeau, and Southwest Missouri at Springfield. Northeastern Missouri at Kirksville changed its name to Truman State University in 1996.

Students in science class

Lincoln University at Jefferson City was founded immediately after the Civil War by black soldiers who had served in the U.S. Colored Infantry. It became a state college in 1890, and achieved university status within thirty years. It has long attracted white students as well as African-Americans.

Preacher Defies Ban

The Reverend John Berry Meachum, a former slave and preacher, defied an 1847 Missouri state law that prohibited blacks from being educated in the state. He got around the rule by starting the Freedom School on a steamboat anchored in the middle of the Mississippi River, just off St. Louis. This brought the school under federal jurisdiction, exempting it from Missouri's laws. Meachum purchased the release of his family from slavery and helped other blacks to become free by helping them learn a trade so that they could earn a living. ■

Along with several junior colleges within the state, Missouri Western State College at St. Joseph and Missouri Southern State College at Joplin are additional places to earn higher degrees. There are also more than twenty private colleges, most of which were founded by religious organizations. Washington University in St. Louis, however, was founded without religious affiliation. It was started by the grandfather of poet T. S. Eliot and originally was called Eliot Seminary. Numerous Nobel Prize-winning scientists have been associated with the university, and it has one of the nation's leading medical schools.

For a long time, even during the progressive era of the early 1900s, the education of children was sometimes sacrificed in the interest of business. Child labor was an accepted fact for generations, with children as young as seven years old working at back-breaking jobs. Many children, especially those from poorer families, had no access to schools. Others simply had to work to help their families survive hard times. Today, problems like drug abuse, juvenile crime, and divorce plague some of Missouri's children. But public education has greatly improved since the early days on the frontier when untrained teachers did the best they could in one-room schoolhouses.

Chapter Ten

Poets, Painters, and Players

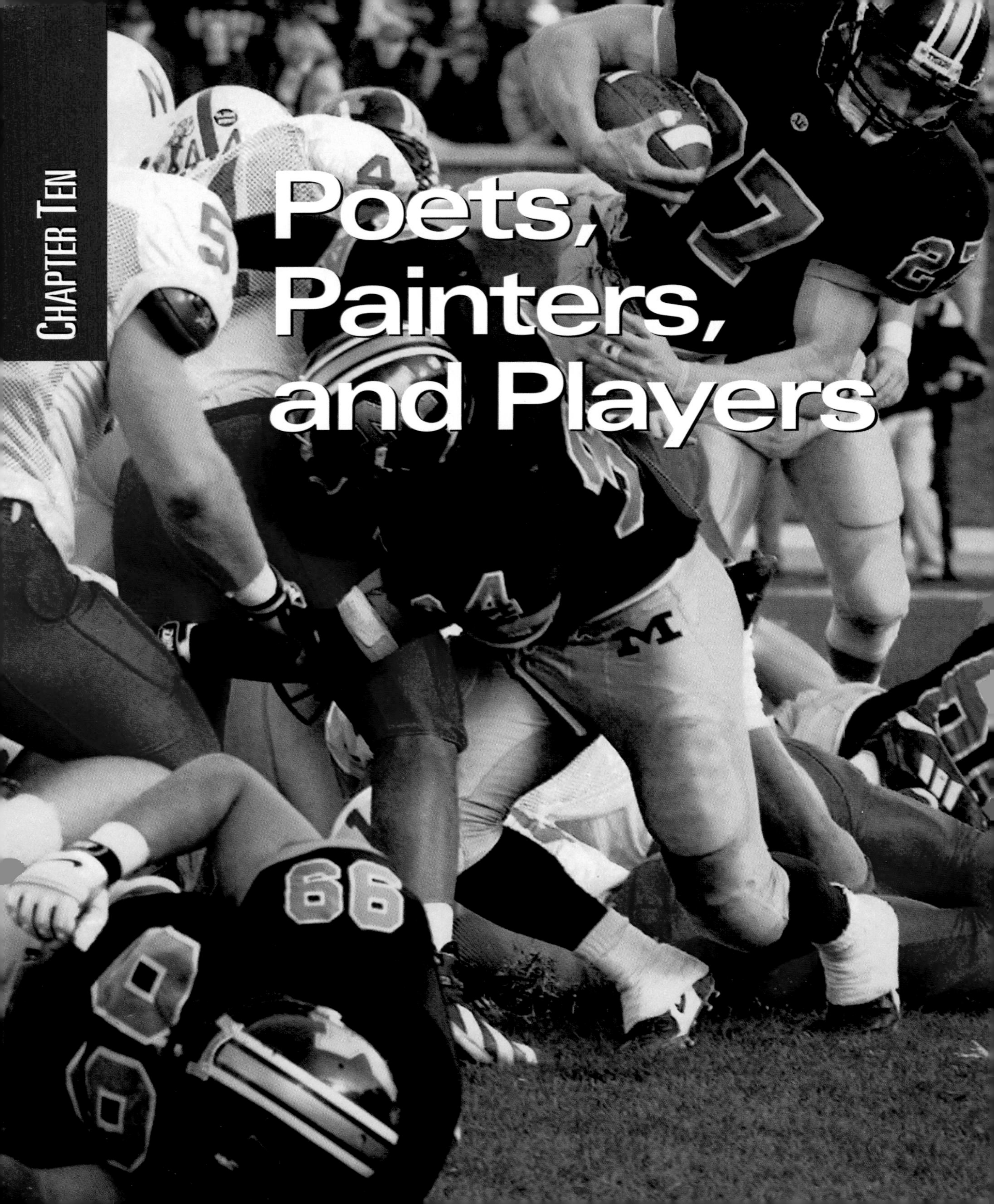

Missouri's rolling hills, fast-moving rivers, brilliant sunrises and sunsets, productive farms, and bustling cities have always inspired the state's artistic community. Missouri has been a creative cradle for poets, novelists, painters, musicians, sculptors, photographers, and dancers. Athletes, too, have found a fertile field here.

Samuel Clemens, or Mark Twain

The Mighty Pen

Probably one of the most famous Missourians was author and humorist Mark Twain. Mark Twain is the pen name of Samuel Langhorne Clemens. He took this name during the three years he worked as a riverboat pilot on the Mississippi. *Mark twain* is a riverboat term meaning "two fathoms," or 12 feet (3.7 m). Twain was born in Florida, Missouri, in 1835, and died in Connecticut in 1910. Growing up in the Mississippi River town of Hannibal, he collected childhood memories that inspired his *Tom Sawyer* (1876) and *The Adventures of Huckleberry Finn* (1884).

Missouri must bring out the poetry in people. The state, especially St. Louis, has been the home of an abundance of poets. Sara Teasdale (1884–1933) was best known for her simple, thoughtful lyrics. The notable T. S. Eliot (1888–1965), author of *The Wasteland,* was the winner of the 1948 Nobel Prize for literature. He may be best known by the general public for the poems about cats that served as the basis for the long-running Broadway musical

Opposite: A University of Missouri football game

T. S. Eliot

Cats. Eugene Field (1850–1895) was primarily a journalist, but made his lasting name by writing such poems as "Little Boy Blue," about the death of a child.

The state also has two Pulitzer Prize–winners in poetry. Marianne Craig Moore (1887–1972), who was born in St. Louis, won in 1952. Howard Nemerov (1920–1991) of Washington University won the Pulitzer in 1978. He was named poet laureate of the United States in 1988. Mona Van Duyn (1921–), also of Washington University, became the U.S. poet laureate in 1992, the first woman to be named to that prestigious position.

Missouri has also produced some fine African-American poets. Award-winning Langston Hughes (1902–1967) hailed from Joplin. His first published poem was *The Negro Speaks of Rivers*. Maya Angelou (1928–) read one of her poems at the inauguration of President Bill Clinton. In addition to poetry, she has written a series of beautiful autobiographical books, as well as a children's book.

The Performing Arts

Kansas City can boast that it is the home of the State Ballet of Missouri, as well as the Lyric Opera and the Kansas City Symphony. The Midland Center for the Performing Arts is housed in a refurbished 1928 movie theater, which provides an elegant setting for touring Broadway plays and concerts. The Folly Theater is the most colorful performing hall in Kansas City. Once a bustling burlesque house, it endured tough times until it was renovated in 1981 at a cost of $4.4 million. Now listed on the National Register of Historic Places, it hosts musicals, children's shows, and a range of other entertainment.

For the summertime set, Swope Park's outdoor Starlight Theatre in Kansas City presents plays and concerts under the moon. The St. Louis Black Repertory Company uses the slogan "Black by Popular Demand." The troupe presents works by noted African-American playwrights in the Grandel Square Theater located in the city's Grand Center Arts and Entertainment District.

Kids who love theater also have plenty of outlets in Missouri. Kansas City has two children's acting companies. The Coterie Children's Theater was organized in 1973, and the Theatre for Young America opened in 1977. From its Columbia base, Teen-to-Teen Theater was formed in 1992. It travels statewide to help young people learn how to deal with the consequences of high-risk behavior involving sex, drugs, and alcohol. The troupe's short plays are written by the teens, who encourage their audiences to talk about these challenging issues.

Talking Jazz and More

When talking jazz, music aficionados talk "Missouri." More specifically, they talk about the rollicking, hot-licks St. Louis and Kansas City scene. For generations, both cities have nurtured the best in this swinging, upbeat sound in small nightclubs, church basements, and concert halls. The Kansas City Jazz Commission heavily promotes shows by local and international stars, as well as the Jazz Hall of Fame. The city's Jazz and Blues Festival presents free summertime shows that attract visitors from around the world.

Ragtime

Scott Joplin (1868–1917) was a St. Louis musician known as the "King of Ragtime." Joplin was an accomplished pianist who produced numerous snappy, foot-tapping scores, including "The Maple Leaf Rag" and an opera, *Tremonisha*. Interest in his music received a boost when one of his pieces, "The Entertainer," was adapted as the film score for the 1973 movie *The Sting*.

Joplin spent much of his life in Sedalia. He was a student at George R. Smith College there and worked with music publisher John S. Stark. Scott Joplin's home in St. Louis is now maintained as a museum and a state historic site. ■

The Charlie Parker Memorial Foundation of Kansas City is named after the city's favorite musical son—the famed saxophone player whose nickname was "Bird" or "Yardbird." It also sponsors jazz performances, harking back to the days when more than fifty lively music clubs lined the city's Twelfth Street.

W. C. Handy

One of the most famous St. Louis jazz greats was W. C. Handy. He was born in Alabama and lived in Memphis and New York. But, in 1914, he composed "St. Louis Blues," now the theme song for the St. Louis Blues hockey team. Josephine Baker was another noted jazz performer whose golden voice delighted audiences. She was born in St. Louis in 1906 but lived abroad most of her life and died in 1975 in Paris.

Not only jazz but other forms of music have long been popular in Missouri. Bobby McFerrin was the first African-American to perform regularly at the Metropolitan Opera. Rhythm-and-blues artist Angela Winbush has recorded dozens of songs. And rock and roll great Chuck Berry was born and raised in St. Louis.

The St. Louis Symphony is one of the oldest orchestras in the United States, celebrating its 121st season in 2000. It frequently commissions fine composers to create works especially for that orchestra.

Brush to Canvas

In the art world, Missouri has been the cradle of an impressive list of famous painters. Thomas Hart Benton (1889–1975), grandnephew of the famous Missouri senator, became known across the country for his murals–giant paintings on the walls of public buildings. In 1935, the tobacco-chewing, argumentative artist returned home to Missouri to paint a mural in the legislature's lounge in the State Capitol. His sprawling scenes include many colorful characters from the state's stormy past. They range from political boss Tom Pendergast to outlaw Jesse James.

Spencer Taylor and Solomon Thurman created another famous Missouri mural—*Black Americans in Flight*—at Lambert St. Louis International Airport. It depicts the achievements of African-American fliers from 1917 to the present.

The state has a long tradition of community aid for the arts, with an active Missouri Arts Board helping up-and-coming and established artists. The St. Louis Artists' Guild is more than a century old. It holds workshops and exhibitions for the public and lectures for its members.

Internationally Known Museums

The state's museums are internationally known. The Nelson-Atkins Museum of Art in Kansas City is the eighth-largest such museum in the United States, containing 50,000 items. Among them are numerous Oriental paintings and artifacts, as well as bronze sculptures by contemporary artist Henry Moore. Outside, guests love strolling through the Sculpture Gardens with its 17 acres (6.9 ha) of monumental works by internationally known sculptors.

The St. Louis Art Museum is also considered one of the top ten such facilities in the United States, with its extensive displays

The Great Western Painter

Perhaps the most famous painter of the Old West was Missouri's George Catlin (1796–1872). Born in Wilkes-Barre, Pennsylvania, he grew up on stories about Native Americans and their traditions. As a youngster, many of his friends were frontiersmen.

Catlin journeyed west in the 1830s and began his life's work of recording the images of the Native Americans who lived there. He traveled constantly, but he built his permanent studio in St. Louis. Catlin sketched the clothes and lifestyles of the many different Indian peoples and collected many artifacts. He gave the leaders of the Indian nations a dignity in art that they were rarely given in life. Many of his works are hanging in the Smithsonian Institution, the Catlin Gallery in the National Museum, and the American Museum of Natural History, all in Washington, D.C.

of expressionist and modern art. The building is guarded at the front entrance by the 47-foot (14.3-m) statue of St. Louis the King of France, after whom the city was named. Many of the exhibits highlight work by minority artists. The museum is one of the few buildings that remain from the 1904 Louisiana Purchase Exposition.

Missouri on Film

Missouri's landscape is often used in commercials and films. The St. Louis Film Office actively courts Hollywood companies. The best-known Missourian in the film world was director John Huston (1906–1987), who was born in Nevada, Missouri. His extensive credits include such classics as *The Maltese Falcon* and *Treasure of the Sierra Madre*. Another major film director and screenwriter, Robert Altman, was born in Kansas City in 1925. He even titled one of his feature films after his hometown. *Kansas City*, produced in 1996, which depicts the fictional kidnapping of a politician's wife by a petty gangster.

Baseball Passion

Missouri has been a baseball state almost since the sport was organized. Nothing equals the crack of a bat against a ball, the cheer of the crowds, and an old-fashioned hot dog during a game. The state's stellar stars include fast-talking baseball manager Casey Stengel (1890–1975) and pitcher Jay Hanna ("Dizzy") Dean (1911–1974).

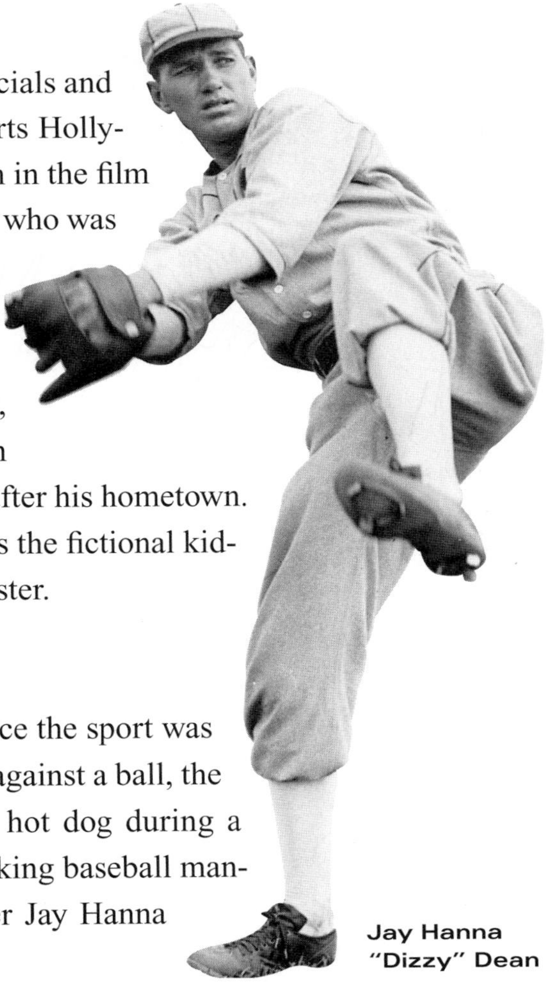

Jay Hanna "Dizzy" Dean

70 for the Record Book

Everyone knew that the St. Louis Cardinals' Mark McGwire was good when the team acquired him from the Oakland Athletics, but no one knew *how* good . . . until the summer of 1998. Sports fans around the world watched the first baseman in a home-run competition with the Chicago Cubs' Sammy Sosa. They matched each other home run for home run, until late in the season. Then McGwire took the lead and kept it. After breaking Roger Maris's 37-year-home-run record of sixty-one for a season, McGwire went on and hit a glorious seventy. Cardinals fans didn't even care that the team itself was losing that year—Mark McGwire made everything all right! ■

Kansas City is home to the American League's Royals baseball club and St. Louis fans love watching the National League's St. Louis Cardinals in Busch Stadium. The Cardinals have won the World Series eight times since 1926. Adjacent to Busch Stadium is the team's Hall of Fame, which is packed with artifacts. The Negro League Baseball Museum in Kansas City opened in 1997.

Something for Everyone

Kansas Citians are also proud of their Chiefs football club; the Blades minor-league hockey team; the Attack, a National Professional Soccer League club for indoor matches; and the Wizards, a pro outdoor team. Fans attend indoor events at the $23 million Kemper Arena. Many other events are held in the $71 million Harry S. Truman Sports Complex, the world's only side-by-side football and baseball stadiums.

It's also easy to visit sports attractions in St. Louis. Across the street from the city's Busch Stadium is the National Bowling Hall of Fame. Not far away is the Kiel Center, which hosts the

Opposite: Tamarick Vanover of the Kansas City Chiefs

Great Despite Segregation

Famed baseball pitcher LeRoy (Satchel) Paige (1906?–1982) was born in Mobile, Alabama, but spent much of his playing life in Missouri. Because of segregation, which did not allow black and white players to play together, he had to pitch for the Negro Southern Association and the Negro National League. Paige played with the Kansas City Monarchs, which earned the Negro National League championship in 1941. He also pitched for the Kansas City Athletics and the St. Louis Browns. Through his career, he played in more than 2,500 games and helped win at least 2,000. He pitched 250 shut-outs and more than forty no-hit games.

After Satchel Paige retired to his home in St. Louis, he continued playing in exhibition games around the United States. Always good for a quote, one of his famous sayings was, "Don't look back, something might be gaining on you." He always claimed he never knew his exact age because, he joked, the family goat ate his birth certificate. In 1971, Paige was inducted into the National Baseball Hall of Fame. ■

exciting St. Louis Blues hockey club of the National Hockey League.

Missouri sports fans are an active bunch. In addition to numerous college and high school teams, there are amateur, youth, adult, and senior leagues in many sports. The more energetic Missourians can select from basketball, baseball, soccer, hockey, tennis, golf, swimming, parachuting, hang-gliding, rugby, rollerblading, rowing, skiing and a host of other athletic endeavors. There is even Women on Wheels, a female motorcycle club that tours on weekends and sponsors many community benefits.

Whether as spectator or participant, Missouri has an art or sport for everyone.

Timeline

United States History

1607 The first permanent English settlement is established in North America at Jamestown.

1620 Pilgrims found Plymouth Colony, the second permanent English settlement.

1776 America declares its independence from Britain.

1783 The Treaty of Paris officially ends the Revolutionary War in America.

1787 The U.S. Constitution is written.

1803 The Louisiana Purchase almost doubles the size of the United States.

1812–15 U.S and Britain fight the War of 1812.

Missouri State History

1673 Louis Jolliet and Jacques Marquette canoe down Mississippi River i what is now Missouri.

1682 René-Robert Cavelier, Sieur de La Salle, claims for France all land drained by Mississippi River.

ca. 1735 Ste. Genevieve, Missouri's first permanent white settlement, is established.

1764 St. Louis is founded by Pierre Laclède.

1800 The French regain control of Louisiana from the Spanish under the Treaty of San Ildefonso.

1803 Missouri comes under the control of the United States.

1812 Missouri becomes a territory. A governor is appointed and a House of Representatives is elected.

1821 Missouri becomes the twenty-fourth state on August 10.

United States History

1861–65 The North and South fight each other in the American Civil War.

1917–18 The United States is involved in World War I.

1929 The stock market crashes, plunging the United States into the Great Depression.

1941–45 The United States fights in World War II.

1945 The United States becomes a charter member of the United Nations.

1951–53 The United States fights in the Korean War.

1964 The U.S. Congress enacts a series of groundbreaking civil rights laws.

1964–73 The United States engages in the Vietnam War.

1991 The United States and other nations fight the brief Persian Gulf War against Iraq.

Missouri State History

1855 Fighting breaks out along the Missouri–Kansas border between Missourians in favor of slavery and Kansans against it.

1861 Missouri forces are defeated in the Battle of Booneville during the American Civil War.

1951 The Missouri River floods and destroys Kansas City's packing industry.

1973 Missouri purchases St. Louis's Wainwright Building, considered by many to be the first American skyscraper.

1984 Harriet Woods is elected lieutenant governor, the highest office ever filled by a woman in Missouri.

Fast Facts

Bluebird

Flowering dogwood

Statehood date	August 10,1821, the 24th state
Origin of state name	From the Fox language for another tribe called *Oumessourit*, meaning "Big Canoe People"
State capital	Jefferson City
State nickname	Show-Me State
State motto	*Salus Populi Suprema Lex Esto* (The welfare of the people shall be the supreme law)
State bird	Eastern bluebird
State flower	Hawthorn blossom
State stone	Mozarkite
State mineral	Galena (lead)
State song	"Missouri Waltz "
State tree	Flowering dogwood
State fair	Third week in August at Sedalia
Total area; rank	69,709 sq. mi. (180,546 sq km); 21st

Mississippi River

Land; rank	68,896 sq. mi. (178,441 sq km); 18th
Water; rank	811 sq. mi. (2,100 sq km); 32nd
***Inland water;* rank**	811 sq. mi. (2,100 sq km); 26th
Geographic center	Miller, 20 miles (32 km) southwest of Jefferson City
Latitude and longitude	Missouri is located approximately between 36° and 40° 35' N and 85° 5' and 95° 45' W
Highest point	Taum Sauk Mountain 1,772 feet (540 m)
Lowest point	St. Francis River, 230 feet (70 m)
Largest city	Kansas City
Number of counties	114
Population; rank	5,137,804 (1990 census); 15th
Density	74 persons per sq. mi. (28 per sq km)
Population distribution	69% urban, 31% rural

Ethnic distribution (does not equal 100%)	White	87.67%
	African-American	11.42%
	Hispanic	1.21%
	Asian and Pacific Islanders	0.81%
	Native American	0.20%
	Other	0.42%

Record high temperature	118°F (48°C) at Clinton on July 15,1936, at Lamar on July 18, 1936, and at Union and Warsaw on July 14, 1954
Record low temperature	–40°F (–40°C) at Warsaw on February 13, 1905

Dred Scott

Average July temperature	78°F (26°C)
Average January temperature	30°F (–1°C)
Average annual precipitation	40 inches (102 cm)

Natural Areas and Historic Sites

National Monument

George Washington Carver National Monument was established in 1943 and is dedicated to the famous humanitarian and scientist. It is located on the site of the Moses Carver farm, where George Washington Carver was born into slavery and later orphaned.

National Historic Sites

Harry S. Truman

Harry S. Truman National Historic Site consists of the Truman Home in Independence and the Truman Farm House in Grandview. Visitors can see the history of the thirty-third president of the United States.

Ulysses S. Grant National Historic Site in St. Louis honors the American Civil War general and his wife, Julia Denton Grant. A house, stone building, barn, and other buildings stand on the 9.65-acre (4 ha) site.

National Memorial

Jefferson National Expansion Memorial, also known as the *Gateway Arch,* is one of the most famous national memorials in the country. It was built in honor of President Jefferson's efforts to expand the United States westward. Tourists can ride up the 630-foot (192 m) structure and to the observation room for breathtaking views.

Ozark Mountains

National Scenic Riverway

Ozark National Scenic Riverway includes the narrow river path along the Jacks Fork and Current Rivers, and is the nation's first official riverway.

National Battlefield

Wilson's Creek National Battlefield in Republic is the site of the first American Civil War battle west of the Mississippi River. People should have little trouble feeling as if they are in the nineteenth century, as the land and structures have hardly changed since the original battle.

National Historic Trail

Lewis & Clark National Historic Trail covers 3,700 miles (5,954 km) through eleven states, including Missouri. Visitors of the trail can follow the explorers' route, finding out for themselves why the two men returned to President Jefferson in awe of nature's majesty.

National Forests

Mark Twain National Forest is the only national forest in Missouri. It covers 1.5 million acres (0.6 million ha) of the southern part of the state and has many different landforms, such as deep valleys, vast plains, streams, and lakes.

State Parks

Bennett Spring in Lebanon boasts the third largest spring in the state, out of which 100 million gallons (378.5 million liters) of water flow daily. This is one of Missouri's most visited state parks.

Elephant Rocks in Belleview has rock formations more than 1 billion years old. This park also offers visually impaired tourists a trail with Braille guides—the first such trail in the nation.

Ha Ha Tonka in Camdenton is one of the state's most beautiful parks. Sightseers will enjoy the many different types of topography, such as the limestone bluffs that overlook Lake of the Ozarks and karst land (a mixture of caves, sinkholes, underground streams, springs, and natural bridges). Adding mystery to the blend are the remnants of a stone castle.

Elephant Rocks State Park

Johnson's Shut-Ins in Middlebrook consists partly of large gorges, or shut-ins, that have formed from the Black River cutting through the oldest exposed rock in the United States. More than 1,000 species of flowers and plants grow in this wilderness park, which is one of the beginning points of the Ozark Trail.

Mark Twain State Park in Stoutsville is in the Salt River Hills, north of the Missouri River, next to Mark Twain Lake.

Roaring River State Park offers great views of the Ozarks. The river after which the 3,403-acre (1,378 ha) park is named is created from a spring, and visitors can watch a waterfall flow down the mountain into the river.

Sports Teams

NCAA Teams (Division 1)

St. Louis University Billikens

Southeast Missouri State University Bears

University of Missouri-Columbia Tiger

University of Missouri-Kansas City Kangaroos

Major League Baseball

St. Louis Cardinals

Kansas City Royals

National Football League

Kansas City Chiefs

National Hockey League

St. Louis Blues

Major League Soccer

Kansas City Wizards

Kansas City Chiefs

Cultural Institutions

Libraries

The Harry S. Truman Library in Independence is part of the Harry S. Truman National Historic Site. It contains more than 3 million documents and memoranda from Truman's presidency.

The Missouri State Library, built in 1946 in Jefferson City, holds the state archives.

The Pius XII Memorial Library at the St. Louis University has a collection of microfilmed documents from the Vatican Library.

Westminster College's *Winston Churchill Memorial Library* in Fulton honors the British prime minister who delivered his famous Iron Curtain speech on campus in 1946.

Museums

The *Missouri Historical Society* in St. Louis contains a collection of works relating to Charles Lindbergh's 1927 solo flight across the Atlantic Ocean.

Missouri state capitol

The *Nelson-Atkins Museum of Art* in Kansas City is one of the ten largest art museums in the United States. It is particularly noted for its collection of East Asian art.

The state capitol in Jefferson City has a museum with many reminders of Missouri's past.

The *St. Louis Art Museum* has 30,000 works of art, including an Egyptian mummy that is 3,000 years old and an X ray that allows people see inside the mummy's case.

The *Toy and Miniature Museum*, located at the University of Missouri-Kansas City, has twenty-four rooms filled with antique dolls, doll houses, toys, and trains.

Performing Arts

Missouri has two major opera companies, two symphony orchestras, one dance company, and one professional theater company.

Universities and Colleges

In the mid-1990s, Missouri had 30 public and 71 private institutions of higher learning.

Annual Events

January–March

Cabin Fever Quilt Show in Independence (February)

State trout season opening in Montauk State Park (March 1)

April–June

Dogwood Festival in Camdenton (April)

Pony Express celebration in St. Joseph (April)

Jesse James celebration in St. Joseph (April)

Turkey-calling championships in Kirksville (April)

Maifest in Hermann (May)

Storytelling Festival in St. Louis (May)

Valley of Flowers Festival in Florissant (May)

Riverfest at Cape Girardeau (June)

Scott Joplin Ragtime Festival in Sedalia (June)

July–September

Bluegrass Festival at Sam A. Baker State Park in Patterson (July)

National Tom Sawyer Days in Hannibal (July)

Fair St. Louis (July)

Bastille Days in Ste. Genevieve (July)

Country Club Plaza

Ozark Empire Fair in Springfield (August)

State Fair in Sedalia (August)

Cotton Carnival in Sikeston (September)

Country Club Plaza Art Fair in Kansas City (September)

Great Forest Park Balloon Race in St. Louis (September)

National Festival of Craftsmen in Silver Dollar City (September–October)

October–December

Fête d'Automne in Old Mines (October)

Oktoberfest in Hermann (October)

American Royal Livestock, Horse Show, and Rodeo in Kansas City (November)

Ozark Mountain Christmas near Branson (November–December)

Jay Hanna "Dizzy" Dean

Famous People

Josephine Baker (1906–1975)	Entertainer
Chuck Berry (1926–)	Singer
George Washington Carver (1861–1943)	Agronomist and chemist
Jay Hanna "Dizzy" Dean (1911–1974)	Baseball Pitcher
Samuel Langhorne Clemens (Mark Twain) (1835–1910)	Humorist and author
Charlie Parker (1920–1955)	Jazz saxophonist
James Cash Penney (1875–1971)	Merchant
Thomas Stearns (T. S.) Eliot (1888–1965)	Poet and critic
Harry S. Truman (1884–1972)	U.S. president

To Find Out More

History

- Doherty, Craig A. *The Gateway Arch*. Woodbridge, Conn.: Blackbirch Marketing, 1995.
- Fradin, Dennis Brindell. *Missouri*. Danbury, Conn.: Childrens Press, 1994.
- Harkrader, Lisa. *Kidding around Kansas City: What to Do, Where to Go, and How to Have Fun in Kansas City*. Santa Fe, N.M.: John Muir Publications, 1997.
- Ladoux, Rita C. *Missouri*. Minneapolis: Lerner Publications Company, 1991.
- Lourie, Peter. *In the Path of Lewis and Clark: Traveling the Missouri*. New York: Silver Burdett, 1997.
- Thompson, Kathleen. *Missouri*. Austin, Tex.: Raintree/Steck Vaughn, 1996.

Fiction

- Twain, Mark. *The Adventures of Huckleberry Finn*. Illus. by Steven Kellogg. New York: William Morrow & Company, 1994.
- Twain, Mark. *The Adventures of Tom Sawyer*. Illus. by Donald McKay. New York: Grosset & Dunlap, 1994.

Biographies

- Faber, Doris. *Calamity Jane: Her Life and Her Legend*. New York: Houghton Mifflin Co., 1997.

- Green, Carl R. and William R. Sandford. *Jesse James.* Springfield, N.J.: Enslow Publishers, Inc., 1992.
- Nicholson, Lois P. and William Epes. *George Washington Carver.* Broomall, Penn.: Chelsea House Publishers, 1994.
- Wilder, Laura Ingalls. *On the Way Home.* New York: HarperCollins Juvenile Books, 1962.

Websites

- **Missouri State Library**
  http://www.mosl.sos.state.mo.us/lib-ser/libser.html
  To look at information about the official resource center for the state
- **State of Missouri**
  http://www.state.mo.us
  The official website of Missouri
- **The St. Louis Art Museum**
  http://www.slam.org
  To find out about special exhibits, collections, location, and hours

Addresses

- **Missouri Historical Society Museum**
  5700 Lindell
  St. Louis, MO 63112
  To see photos, documents, and other pieces of Missouri's past
- **Missouri Division of Tourism**
  P.O. Box 1055
  Jefferson City, MO 65102
  To find information about different travel destinations within Missouri
- **Governor's Office**
  P.O. Box 720, Missouri State Capitol
  Room 217B
  Jefferson City, MO 65102
  To contact Missouri's highest elected official

Index

Page numbers in *italics* indicate illustrations.

Meet the Author

Martin Hintz has been a regular visitor to Missouri for years. He has taken photography workshops in the Ozark Mountains, attended formal dinners in St. Louis, driven the state's freeways, watched Mississippi River floodwaters, eaten Kansas City barbecue, listened to jazz music in bars and church basements, traveled to the top of the St. Louis arch, interviewed Missouri politicians, and tracked the footsteps of outlaw Jesse James.

The state is one of his favorites, for its fishing, hiking, photography, and canoeing opportunities. On several expeditions, he was accompanied by his children—Dan, Steve, and Kate. Each had plenty of insights as to what makes Missouri great.

To gather information for *America the Beautiful: Missouri,* Hintz not only visited the state many times but used library and Internet resources. In addition, many of his friends in the Missouri travel industry sent information about their communities. He also talked with state officials, historians, political leaders, teachers, and students about their state. Various state departments and commissions sent background on Missouri, covering everything from the mining industry to state forests to population density to the size of mules.

Chairman of the Central States Chapter of the Society of American Travel Writers, Hintz has written dozens of travel and guide books and hundreds of magazine and newspaper articles. Many of his books have won awards. In addition to his writing, Hintz publishes *The Irish American Post.* His news journal covers both national and international affairs of interest to the Irish and Irish American community, with offices in London, Dublin, and Belfast. Hintz has written many stories about Missouri's business, educational, and political connections with Ireland. He regularly visits Irish communities in the state for features and news stories.

Hintz lives in River Hills, Wisconsin, a suburb of Milwaukee, with his wife, Pam Percy, a producer for Wisconsin Public Radio. They have fifteen chickens, two turkeys, and five ducks on their mini-farm.

Photo Credits

Photographs ©:

AllSport USA: 6 bottom, 124 (Jed Jacobsohn)

Aneal S. Vohra: 73, 102, 104

AP/Wide World Photos: 51, 53, 116 (James A. Finley), 90 (Kelley McCall), 42, 46, 47, 49 bottom, 50, 85, 86, 117, 130, 125, 132 bottom (Ed Zurga)

Bob Clemenz Photography: 15

Carol L. House Photography: 13, 81, 111, 112

Corbis-Bettmann: 28 (Library of Congress), 44 bottom, 49 top, 87, 123, 135 bottom (UPI), 6 top right, 17, 32, 36, 45, 71, 118, 120, 129 bottom

Courtesy of State Historical Society of Missouri, Columbia: 29 (Saukie and Fox Indians, engraving by George Catlin), 20 (Old Saint Genevieve, mural by Oscar Berninghaus, Missouri State Capitol), 21 (Early Lead Mining, mural by Oscar Berninghaus, Missouri State Capitol), 44 top (J. J. Wheeldon)

Dave G. Houser: 6 top left, 100, 107

Dembinsky Photo Assoc.: 94 left, 128 bottom (Bill Lea), 60, 132 top (G. Alan Nelson)

Ed Cooper Enterprises: 14

Envision: 77 (Steven Needham)

Folio, Inc.: 101 (David R. Frazier)

Gamma-Liaison, Inc.: 7 top left, 109 bottom (Barry King), 103, 114 (Ed Lallo)

Gene Ahrens: cover

Michael Sharp: 92

Missouri Department of Natural Resources: 2 (Paul Nelson), 56 (Eugene Vale)

Missouri Division of Tourism: 7 top right, 95 (Conservation Department), 97

Missouri Historical Society: 18, 19

Missouri State Archives: 66 (Mark Wright), 27, 40

New England Stock Photo: 98 (Don Hamerman)

North Wind Picture Archives: 11, 23, 25, 26, 33

Photo Researchers: 7 top center, 55, 129 top (Max & Bea Hunn)

Randall Hyman: 69

Root Resources: 68 (James Blank), 7 bottom, 94 right, 128 top (Richard Jacobs)

Sherry Farrell: 84

Stock Montage, Inc.: 122 (The Newberry Library), 12, 31, 34, 37, 38, 39, 41, 43, 109 top

The Historic New Orleans Collections: 22 (1981.134)

Tom Dietrich: 8, 74, 83, 135 top

Tom Till: back cover, 6 top center, 9, 80

Tony Stone Images: 78, 133 (Doris De Witt), 75 (Donovan Reese)

Unicorn Stock Photos: 64, 96 (Eric R. Berndt), 82, 99 (Paul A. Hein), 59 (Karen Holsinger Mullen), 54, 131 (Andre Jenny), 76 (Jim Shippee), 106 (Aneal V. Vohra), 62 (John Ward)

Maps by XNR Productions, Inc.